ONE STEP AT A TIME

Buddhist Meditation for Absolute Beginners

Phra Peter Pannapadipo

POST
BOOKS

One Step at a Time: Buddhist Meditation
for Absolute Beginners
Published by Post Books, The Post Publishing Plc.
136 Na Ranong Road, off Sunthorn Kosa Road
Klong Toey, Bangkok 10110, Thailand
Tel. (662) 240-3700 ext. 1691-2
Fax. (662) 671-9698
e-mail: postbooks@bangkokpost.net
http: //www.bangkokpost.net/postbooks/

© Phra Peter Pannapadipo 1998

First published in Thailand in November 1998
Second printing 2000
Printed by Allied Printers, The Post Publishing Plc.

National Library of Thailand Cataloging-in-Publication Data
Phra Peter Pannapadipo
One Step at a Time: Buddhist Meditation
for Absolute Beginners. -- 2nd printing --
Bangkok : Post Books, 2000. 168 p.
1. Buddhist meditation. I. Title.
294.3122

ISBN : 974-202-030-2

Cover design: Chaiyos Thongsim
Page setup: Orraphin Pratummaneesuk
Illustrations: Raknawee Poonwong
Set in: Garamond and Futura

"*Try to be mindful and let things take their natural course. Then the mind will become still in any surroundings, like a clear forest pool. All kinds of wonderful, rare animals will come to drink at the pool, and you will clearly see the nature of all things. You will see many strange and wonderful things come and go, but you will be still. This is the happiness of the Buddha.*"

Phra Acharn Chah Subhaddo

Contents

Preface

After publication of my first book, *Phra Farang: An English Monk in Thailand*, I received many hundreds of letters from Western readers asking questions about Buddhism, about my life as a monk and, particularly, about my own meditation practice. Many of the writers said that they practised meditation in one form or another, but frequently with little apparent benefit and often without ever having had any formal instruction. Most of my correspondents had a good – if sometimes vague – idea of the aims of Buddhist meditation, but frequently seemed to find the practice too difficult or simply too boring. They struggled along in fits and starts, not really getting anywhere. Other readers said that they wanted to start to practise meditation, but even in Southeast Asia found it quite difficult to find an instructor or guide who could teach absolute beginners.

Some years ago my own meditation instructor, Phra Acharn Amara Thera, the Abbot of the Thai monastery in London, asked me to write a simple little "plain language" booklet that could be used as basic guidance for new Western meditation students at the monastery. The Acharn is undoubtedly one of Thailand's wisest and most knowledgeable meditation masters but he knew that, to be fully understood by new Western students, the booklet had to be written by another Western meditator.

The letters I received after publication of *Phra Farang* made it very apparent to me that there were many Westerners living in Thailand, or visiting the country, who might also benefit from some basic guidance in their meditation practice. I decided to revise and enlarge the original little booklet to try to make meditation practice easier for those who do not have easy access to a guide or an instructor. *One Step at a Time* is the result.

This manual is – I hope – different from many other books about meditation. I have tried to present Buddhist meditation in a straightforward and practical way, without making it seem mysterious or elitist. Some of the guidance I offer is *so* basic that it is frequently overlooked or ignored even by very knowledgeable instructors and authors. Yet it is often these most basic "dos and don'ts" that ensure the meditation practice gets off to a positive and productive start and doesn't degenerate into mere habit or some sort of relaxation exercise. However, even with the very basic instruction that I give, it doesn't follow that meditation is easy. It still needs great commitment and effort on the part of the meditator. I think – increasingly – people of all ages and backgrounds are prepared to make that commitment and effort in their personal search for true peace of mind, true freedom.

I have tried many different ways of finding true freedom and peace of mind, from "turning on and dropping out" in the late 60s, to a life ensnared in materialism, self and hedonism in the Thatcher 80s. Except at the most superficial level, none of that worked for me. Meditation did. I now believe there is only one way to genuine and lasting freedom of mind, and that is through meditation.

I hope that your own practice will lead you to the same realisation.

Phra Peter Pannapadipo
Wat Worranatbanpot
September 1998

One step at a time

My own first lesson in meditation came at the end of a 16-week course of lectures about basic Buddhism. The instructor monk explained the principles of walking meditation to the class of about 20 students who were assembled in a large meditation hall. We closed our eyes and, as instructed, began walking slowly from one side of the hall to the other, trying to keep our concentration focused on specific movements of our feet. Unfortunately, we weren't supposed to close our eyes, so we were all soon falling over tables, chairs and each other. The instructor had forgotten to tell us to keep our eyes open.

It may seem obvious that walking meditation cannot be practised very well with closed eyes, but it wasn't obvious to a very naïve class of absolute beginners. Most of us had only ever heard of sitting meditation and we thought meditation was *always* practised with the eyes closed. We laughed the incident off and I forgot about it.

Years later, after I had ordained as a Buddhist monk, I was living in a tiny rural monastery in the north of Thailand. I was very isolated and was undertaking intense meditation over a period of about a year. At one point I found myself in some difficulty and was not at all sure if I was practising wisely, or even productively. Without anybody to whom I could turn for advice, I had to consider for myself very carefully and objectively what I was doing, how my difficulties had arisen, and where my meditation as a whole was leading.

Amongst other things, I realised that my meditation was in danger of becoming an end in itself, rather than the means to an end. It had started to become something that I was in the habit of doing at certain times each day, and I had begun to lose sight of the *why*. I believe that may be a problem for many regular meditators, though they may not always have enough objectivity about their own practice to realise they are stuck in that particular dead-end. To ensure I fully understood what I was doing, and why, I re-read as much as I could of the Buddha's teaching concerning meditation. I compared it with more modern commentaries and meditation manuals to see whether I had strayed from what the original Teacher had taught.

My difficulties were eventually overcome, but as a result I started to re-think much of what I had learned about meditation, or thought I had learned. I decided to start again almost from the beginning, one step at a time, taking absolutely nothing for granted and relying greatly on my own intuition to guide me.

It was during that review of my practice that I remembered the small incident from my first lesson. I decided that as well as examining my mental and spiritual approach to my meditation, I should also carefully examine the practical aspects too. I thought it possible even likely – that in my years of meditation practice I might well have developed unhelpful habits.

I started to study the various positions I used in my meditation – for sitting, standing, lying and walking practice. I wanted to know what physical stresses my body was placed under in the various positions and to find those that were most comfortable but still conducive to my practice. I tried to understand what happened physiologically in the body when different muscle groups and tendons came into use. I gained something of a reputation in the local village as being rather strange, as a result of crawling about on my hands and knees watching how different people moved their legs and feet, closely observing what actually happened in the feet when they made contact with a solid surface during walking meditation. For a time, everybody I met was asked to slowly sit down from a standing position and fold their legs into a meditative posture, so that I could watch the most typical movements involved, not only of the legs and feet but of the hands and arms also.

I thought carefully about the different environments in which I had practised various types of meditation; bedrooms and bathrooms, marble halls and wooden shacks, forests and cities, caves and crematoria. Which environments had seemed most conducive to the meditation of the time, and to my understanding and proficiency of the time? What sort of environments would be most beneficial for the absolute beginner? What were the particular distractions to be aware of in each?

I tried to recall my own early days of practice, when I frequently became bored and distracted after only a few minutes, and was inclined to give up too easily. What were the factors and disciplines which had eventually enabled me to extend my meditation time to an hour, two hours, and occasionally considerably longer without feeling either physical or mental strain?

I thought about other meditators I had known, experienced practitioners and beginners, monks and laypeople, the various problems they had faced and how they overcame them. I thought about what I had noticed about other peoples' meditation practice, and how I could relate that constructively to my own.

I realised how easy it is for an experienced meditator to forget or overlook some very basic points, and to take it for granted that the student already knows – like keeping the eyes open during walking meditation. I tried to think about every aspect of meditation from the standpoint of an absolute beginner and to remember all those things I had discovered for myself that I wished someone had told *me* at the very start of my meditation practice.

Much of this manual is a result of that review. All meditators are different and progress at their own rate; so I should stress that what may work for me, even on a practical basis, may not work as well for other meditators. My review of the various sitting positions, for example, was based mainly on my body and what I found most comfortable and conducive to my own practice. I am tall and thin, so a short, fat person may have to experiment more to find the best positions for his or her own practice. To a very great extent, we all have to find our *own* way, to work *with* our meditation, to investigate and to consider carefully, rather than blindly following what an instructor, guide, fellow practitioner or manual may tell us.

Although I now occasionally conduct meditation classes at various monasteries in Thailand, especially for beginners from Western countries, I do not really consider myself to be a meditation *teacher*. In fact, I do not believe there is much in meditation that can actually be taught, apart from its theory and practical aspects. Buddhist meditation is a system which leads to **self-realisation**; of seeing the Truth within and around ourselves, for ourselves – in an Ultimate, not Relative sense – and for the arising in the mind of what is known as **Insight-Wisdom**. It is the personal discovery or unveiling of our own Buddha nature. Nobody can *teach* self-realisation to anybody else. Even the Buddha declared that he could only point the way. Certainly, there are meditation masters with both a huge store of knowledge and great wisdom. Knowledge can be passed from one intellect to another, but wisdom, when expressed in words, may frequently sound more like foolish nonsense. Insight-Wisdom must arise intuitively through self-development and <u>cannot</u> be obtained intellectually, though of course it is helpful to have an intellectual understanding of theory before actually commencing practice.

Self-realisation, seeing for oneself, *knowing* for oneself, is very different from intellectual understanding, which can often be quite shallow. However, in meditation, until one has actually experienced this 'knowing' the difference can be difficult to understand – except intellectually.

This manual is intended to give the absolute beginner a start in meditation; a start on the path to self-realisation. It is far from easy and it may seem an impossible goal, but there are many other benefits to be gained whilst progressing towards that goal. It takes time, perseverance, great self-discipline and patience.

The most simple exercises in this manual in walking, sitting and lying meditation, as well as the mindfulness exercises, can certainly be practised at home without an instructor or guide. Later sitting and lying exercises become increasingly more complex and higher levels of developed concentration are needed to practise them most productively. But many meditators find that they do not need to practise the more complex exercises at all. Good levels of concentration, awareness and understanding, with the resulting benefits, can be developed from the most simple exercises. Some meditators base their entire practice over many years on just the first sitting exercise, sometimes with apparent and extraordinary results.

Although the earlier exercises can be practised alone, there are very definite advantages in attending regular group meditation classes under the guidance of an experienced instructor. The new meditator practising alone is far more likely to give up too easily or too quickly, and may not always make the effort needed. The support of a group can help generate and sustain that effort.

If you begin to practise more earnestly and with higher goals than those you are likely to start off with, you may also find that you really need wise guidance of the kind that no manual can provide. You should seek it. There are many dead-ends and distractions in meditation – some are very pleasant and meditators may be tempted to halt the practice at that point, thinking they have reached some ultimate 'goal' – but there is only one true path. An experienced guide can not only help keep you from straying from that path but can also move you forward with gradual and systematic progress based on his or her own experience and developed wisdom. As the guide gets to know you and your personality, so your meditation practice can be programmed to suit you as an individual, which becomes increasingly important as concentration levels increase.

There are many very scholarly monks and laypeople teaching meditation, especially in Thailand, but this author is not one of them. I do not read either Pali or Sanskrit, the languages of the earliest Buddhist scriptures, and I must rely on other scholars for their translations of the scriptures and commentaries into English. There are some Pali words that embody whole concepts and which do not always translate easily. All meditators should be familiar with those words and concepts, but it seems to me that there are some Western practitioners and instructors who seem over-fond of using Pali terms. I believe they are frequently unnecessary, especially for absolute beginners. I have avoided them in this manual whenever possible, but I have given them when I think it is helpful. A glossary of such useful terms in Pali and English appears at the end of this manual.

Although I do not consider myself to be a meditation teacher, and I am not a scholar monk, I try to <u>practise</u> what the Buddha taught and to live my life within the guidelines he laid down. And I meditate. I meditate a lot. That's partly at least why I ordained as a Buddhist monk, to give myself the time to do so. Some of what I have learned, even on a practical basis, may be helpful guidance for the beginner.

This is not necessarily a manual just for new Buddhist meditators. Although the meditation techniques described were taught by the man who was known as 'The Buddha' ('The Enlightened One' or 'The Self-Awakened One'), the practice of meditation can bring personal benefits at many different levels to people of any faith. However, whatever the practitioner's personal religious convictions, meditation practice will almost certainly not be beneficial unless it is based on a wholesome moral foundation. In Buddhism, for laypeople, this moral foundation is established by undertaking to keep the 'Five Precepts', or the 'Eight Precepts', the number of precepts depending on the level at which one wishes to practise. (The precepts are detailed later in this manual). The Buddhist moral code for laypeople does not in any way conflict with that of other religions, but for some people it may be helpful not to think of Buddhism as a 'religion' at all. Although over the centuries it has accumulated all the trappings of traditional religion many people, especially Westerners, prefer to think of it as a philosophy, a code of ethics, or simply a life-style.

Different people have different reasons for wanting to practise meditation. You may start off just with the idea that meditation will help you relax or unwind at the end of the day (which it will) but that is practising at the most superficial level – in fact, it isn't really Buddhist meditation at all.

At the other extreme there are people who practise meditation in the hope of developing supernormal, mystic, or even supernatural powers. When I was studying at a meditation centre in England a young man visited the meditation master and explained that he wanted to practise meditation so that he could 'levitate'. I have never seen anybody levitate themselves, though I have frequently heard stories about it. But why should anybody – or any serious meditator with an understanding of the Buddha's teaching – even *want* to? It may be good fun at parties, but it won't take the levitator nearer the real goal of meditation.

Similarly, the Buddhist scholar Dr Walpola Rahula gives an example in his book, *What the Buddha taught*, about a nun in India who through meditation was trying to develop the power of seeing through her ears, even though her normal sight was not impaired. Dr Rahula commented: "This kind of idea is nothing but 'spiritual perversion'. It is always a question of desire, 'thirst' for power."

I suppose if you really want to see through your ears whilst floating several feet above the ground that's fine, but this manual can't tell you how to do it.

Although one does not need to declare oneself Buddhist to practise Buddhist meditation, a background understanding of who the Buddha was and what he taught is helpful. The Buddha taught for 45 years and many aspects of his teaching are profound. In this manual they are explained in the briefest terms and only to the extent necessary to help the beginner's early meditation practice. A list of suggested further reading about the teaching of the Buddha appears at the end of this manual.

2

The Buddha and his teaching

The Buddha was born more than 2,500 years ago. There seems little doubt as to his historical authenticity, but in the succeeding centuries his life-story has become embellished with allegory, fables and miracles. These are fascinating reading, but are ignored in this very brief resume of his life.

Siddhatta* Gotama, who was to become the Buddha, was born in what is now Nepal in about 560BC. In Buddhist traditional histories he was the only son of the ruler of the kingdom of the Sakyas and, as a prince and heir to the throne, he grew up surrounded by luxury and sensual diversions. However, despite the advantages of his birth he realised that the cycle of life was the same for everybody, regardless of wealth or social status: birth, sickness, old age, death. He

* Pali; Sanskrit word: Siddharta might be more common.

also realised that although these natural stages of life were inevitable and brought both physical and mental pain, mankind also suffered from conditioned mental conflict and suffering. He became determined to find the cause and cure of this suffering.

At the age of 29, he left his palace, his wife and new-born son and gave up all the pleasures and privileges of his birth to become a wandering mendicant.

For six years he studied with the most revered and knowledgeable teachers of the time, absorbing all they could teach him of their philosophies and meditation methods. He became a master of Samatha (Concentration) meditation, surpassing even his own teachers. He became an ascetic and practised extreme self-mortification until he was close to death. But he realised that neither the extreme self-indulgence of his life as a prince, nor the extreme self-mortification of the ascetic, could provide the solutions he sought. He understood there had to be what later came to be called The Middle Path of Practice, now usually referred to as **The Middle Way**. But The Middle Way is not just some mid-point between indulgence in, or suppression of, sensual desires. The Middle Way is the method through which we learn to wisely avoid that which is unwholesome and cultivate that which is wholesome.

At the age of 35, Siddhatta Gotama left his teachers and ascetic companions and decided to find his own way. He sat beneath a tree* on the banks of the Neranjara river and started to meditate, determined not to rise until he found the solution to the mental conflict and suffering that all mankind endures.

---

* Since known as the 'Bodhi' or 'Bo' (Wisdom) tree.

When he eventually arose from his meditation he was no longer Siddhatta Gotama. He was 'Fully Awake', he was 'Enlightened', he was 'The Buddha'.

Soon after his Enlightenment the Buddha gave his first sermon to a group of five ascetics, his former companions. The sermon was called 'Setting in motion the Wheel of Truth' and the five ascetics became the Buddha's disciples – the first Buddhist monks.

For 45 years after his Enlightenment the Buddha taught the Dhamma – the natural truths he had realised during his meditation – but he always declared that he only pointed the way and that it was up to each individual to work towards his or her own salvation, just as he had done. 'Dhamma' can be translated as 'that which supports' and is the Truth that each of us can find within ourselves.

The Buddha died* at Kusinara (modern Uttar Pradesh) in India, aged 80. His last exhortation to his monks was to work out their own salvation with diligence.

"Look within", he said, "for thou art Buddha."

Buddhism spread rapidly across India (though it has since largely disappeared in that country), and is now followed in various forms in Thailand, Myanmar (Burma), Sri Lanka, Laos, Cambodia, Vietnam, Tibet, China, Japan, Korea, Mongolia and Taiwan. There is also increasing interest in the West and many study and meditation centres have opened throughout Europe and America.

There are now two main schools of Buddhism: Theravada ('School of the Elders') and Mahayana ('The Great Vehicle'). Though they sometimes appear vastly different in outward

---

* Usually referred to by Buddhists as the 'parinirvana'.

form, the two schools agree on the main principles of the Buddha's teaching. Theravada is the earliest form of Buddhism and is sometimes described as 'primitive' by the later Mahayana School, which includes Zen and Tibetan Vajrayana.

The Teaching

Buddhism is perhaps not a 'religion' in the generally accepted meaning of the word because it does not rely on the concept of a godhead or supreme being in its teaching. The Buddha taught that we must not rely on outside intervention by a god or supreme being, but must instead make the effort ourselves, just as he did.

The Buddha made no claim to divinity, nor even that he was any sort of messenger or prophet of a god. The Buddha was an extraordinary man who, through his own efforts, discovered the path to liberation from suffering. His teaching is neither conjecture nor speculation. It rejects faith, dogma and blind acceptance and instead invites personal investigation and examination, which result in firm conviction based on one's own self-realisation.

Self-realisation is so important in Buddhism that the Buddha told his monks that even *his* teaching should be questioned, and not just blindly accepted because they had faith in him as their teacher. The Buddha said: *"Do not be led by the authority of religious texts, nor by mere logic or inference, nor by considering appearances, nor by delight in speculative opinions, nor by seeming possibilities, nor out of respect for a particular teacher. But when you know for yourselves that certain things are unwholesome and wrong and bad, then give them up.*

And when you know for yourselves that certain things are wholesome and good, then accept them and follow them."

Self-realisation – the personal *knowing* for oneself beyond any doubt; the personal recognition of Ultimate Truth, in which neither logic, religious beliefs nor faith in a particular teacher play any part.

Dukkha

The Buddha said, *"I teach dukkha and the way out of dukkha."*

At the heart of the Buddha's teaching are four statements – the Four Noble Truths – concerning dukkha. 'Truth' in this context means truth which is not just understood intellectually, but which is fully self-realised, and known with an understanding that comes from personal experience and Insight-Wisdom.

Dukkha is a Pali word with no simple or convenient English equivalent, but it is often translated as suffering. Other translations are: unsatisfactoriness, imperfection, mental conflict, anguish, mental pain, anxiety, frustration, or disappointment. Because of the difficulties of translation, the word is usually used in its Pali form.

Briefly, dukkha falls into three categories: 'dukkha-dukkhata' is very close to the English meaning of 'suffering' and covers all the usual physical and mental problems that most people experience from time to time. It is ordinary, everyday suffering, and quite easy to recognise.

'Viparinama-dukkhata' is the suffering caused by change. This type of dukkha is not necessarily obvious until an agreeable or happy state ends, or changes to a disagreeable or unhappy one.

'Sankhara-dukkhata' is suffering caused by ignorance of one's own reality, and the true nature of the world, which leads to craving for and clinging to things or situations which are inherently impermanent. Unless we recognise and accept the impermanent nature of all phenomena we can never free ourselves of this type from suffering.

The Buddha taught that birth is dukkha, sickness is dukkha, aging is dukkha, death is dukkha. All the sorrow, lamentation, grief and despair that everyone feels at some time is dukkha. The Buddha also taught that always wanting to be healthy brings dukkha, always wanting to be young and energetic brings dukkha, and the fear of death brings dukkha. Desire for that which one cannot have, or cannot attain to, brings dukkha. To lose or be separated from the things, situations or people that one likes or loves brings dukkha. To be joined to the things, states or people that one dislikes brings dukkha. Attachment to the idea of a permanent entity – the idea of a 'self' or ego – brings dukkha. Attachment to all impermanent physical or mental states, even joyful ones, brings dukkha. All attachment, all clinging to conditions, situations, people and things will eventually bring dukkha of some kind or other.

Although some of our 'suffering' may be obvious, many people might disagree that life contains quite so much unsatisfactoriness, so much dukkha; and would point to the many simple, joyous and beautiful things to be known, experienced and enjoyed. It is true that life does contain much that seems joyous and pleasurable, but only when viewed at a fairly superficial level. Dukkha can be very subtle. Since all phenomena are impermanent, even joyous experiences or states must change and eventually cease, leaving in their wake our desire to re-experience the same phenomena, or to experience something even better. Whatever it is that we as individuals find pleasurable or satisfying can really give no <u>lasting</u> satisfaction and will simply increase our craving or desire for more of the same.

In the book, 'World Faiths: Buddhism', author Clive Erricker defines dukkha as a "deep-seated internal condition brought about through our relationship with a world that cannot satisfy that which we crave."

The Buddha said that he taught dukkha, but he also taught the way of liberation from dukkha.

The Four Noble Truths
The Four Noble Truths are:
1. There is dukkha.
2. Dukkha arises because of craving (Pali: tanha: craving, greed, delusion, egotistic desire and attachment).
3. Dukkha ceases through the elimination of tanha.
4. The Noble Eightfold Path leads to the elimination of tanha, and hence to the cessation of dukkha.

When reviewing the Four Noble Truths, it is of great importance that their meaning should be fully understood. It is not enough to just accept them intellectually and superficially and say, "Well, yes, I can see that there is a lot of suffering in the world".

When we look at a TV newscast, or read a newspaper, it is easy to see the amount of human misery that exists. But much of what we see and hear through the media, or in our own experience, is frequently just ordinary suffering, no matter how terrible it seems.

The four statements, especially the first, must be reviewed until dukkha is recognised and understood in its most subtle forms. Most people do not appreciate, or tend to mentally ignore or shy away from the fact that dukkha is *potentially* there all the time, in all situations, regardless of whether we think we are having a miserable time or enjoying ourselves. And if we do not *fully* understand and accept that the potential for dukkha is always there, that ignorance and delusion is itself a cause of dukkha.

To investigate dukkha in this way doesn't mean that to practise meditation you first have to become a really depressed person, seeing misery in every aspect of your life. Dukkha should not be understood as 'my' dukkha, something that belongs to oneself. That is not what the first Noble Truth says. The first Noble Truth says that there *is* dukkha. When investigating dukkha, we can use our personal experiences in a dispassionate way to see it in its various guises and most subtle forms, but we should try to understand only that the potential for dukkha is inherent in all things and situations with which we come into contact. It is the reaction of our minds to these phenomena that determines whether that inherent dukkha arises or not. Once this becomes clear – and meditation will make it clear – then we can begin to see the truth of the second and successive statements more clearly.

The Noble Eightfold Path

The Noble Eightfold Path – The Middle Way – leads directly to the eventual goal of all Buddhists: Nibbana

(Nirvana)*: Insight-Wisdom into the true nature of all phenomena, of being able to see everything and every condition as it actually is and, with this perfect understanding, to be able to totally eliminate tanha and hence dukkha.

The eight aspects of the Path are:

1. Right Understanding (or Right View). (Pali: samma ditthi).
2. Right Thought (or Right Attitude). (Pali: samma sankappa).
3. Right Speech. (Pali: samma vaca).
4. Right Action. (Pali: samma kammanta).
5. Right Livelihood. (Pali: samma ajiva).
6. Right Effort. (Pali: samma vayama).
7. Right Mindfulness. (Pali: samma sati).
8. Right Concentration. (Pali: samma samadhi).

'Right' is used in describing the eight aspects of the Path; the word can be understood not only as 'correct', but also to mean the quality in its most perfected form.

The eight aspects of the Path are further grouped as **Morality** (or ethical conduct), which comprises Right Speech, Right Action and Right Livelihood; **Concentration**, comprising Right Effort, Right Mindfulness and Right Concentration, and **Wisdom**, comprising Right Understanding and Right Thought. All three groups, or all eight aspects of the Path, should be developed together, rather than in successive stages.

To practise meditation most effectively, the meditator's life-style must be based on Morality and Concentration.

---

* *Nibbana is the Pali word: Nirvana, the Sanskit one.*

Together these lead to Wisdom, which cannot arise without that dual foundation.

The new practitioner's understanding of the various aspects of the Path will usually initially be based at an intellectual and superficial level, but as he or she 'lives' the Path and gains experience in meditation, so a greater depth of understanding will gradually develop.

The eight aspects of the Path can be explained simply as follows:

1. **Right Understanding** is ultimately the penetrative understanding of things as they really are and not as we perceive them to be, or wish them to be. Right Understanding refers specifically to the Four Noble Truths. Penetrative rather than intellectual understanding comes when the mind has been freed from delusion and has been developed through meditation.

2. **Right Thought** is thought that is free from ill-will to others, free from selfish desire, hatred and violence – the right attitude or outlook on life, in fact. There are three major obstacles to Right Thought: greed, anger and delusionary ignorance, the last being a lack of Insight into the Four Noble Truths.

3. **Right Speech** means not using offensive language, not to lie, gossip or slander, not to use vain, irresponsible or foolish talk, not to be hurtful in one's choice of words and not to use speech prompted by self-interest. Instead, one should always try to be gentle and considerate when talking to, or about, others.

4. **Right Action**: the Five Precepts that Buddhist laypeople use to govern their basic conduct are based on Right

Action. The Five Precepts are: not to take life, not to steal, not to indulge in illicit or adulterous sex, not to lie, and not to lose mindfulness through intoxicating drink or drugs. Instead, the Buddhist tries to develop compassion and love for others, generosity and unselfishness, to develop control over the senses, to be honest when dealing with others and to maintain mindfulness at all times.

5. **Right Livelihood** means avoiding occupations that cause harm to others, such as dealing in drugs, intoxicants, weapons, the slaughter of animals etc.

6. **Right Effort** is the development of will-power to enable one to overcome bad or unwholesome qualities and to cultivate good and wholesome ones. Right Effort is also needed to follow the Eightfold Path and in one's meditation practice.

7. **Right Mindfulness** is to be aware at all times of the actions and activities of the body and mind; to keep control of the senses and not to be led by wrong views and fixed ideas. Right Mindfulness develops through meditation practice.

8. **Right Concentration** is meditation practice and the development of 'one-pointedness' of mind.

Even if one chooses to follow another religion, it can be clearly seen that the development of Morality, Concentration and Wisdom through the Noble Eightfold Path is of benefit not only to oneself, but to others as well.

The training in Wisdom must including an understanding of what are known as the **Three Characteristics of Existence**.

In Pali they are **anicca, dukkha** and **anatta**. As with other aspects of the Buddha's teaching, the Three Characteristics of Existence may at first be understood and accepted only intellectually. It is through meditation that they will be understood more deeply.

The Three Characteristics of Existence

Anicca – 'impermanence'. The Buddha taught that everything is subject to the Law of Cause and Effect: everything that comes into existence must eventually cease to exist. Everything is the creation of preceding causes and, in turn, is the cause of later effects. Everything exists only temporarily and there is <u>nothing</u> that has any permanence.

Dukkha – 'suffering'. Since everything is subject to continual change and decay, clinging to impermanent things or states can only give rise to dukkha of one kind or another, and to one degree or another.

Anatta – 'no self'. The Buddha taught that since all things are impermanent there can be no permanent, unchanging or immortal entity which we can call a 'self' or 'soul'. It is the deluded belief in a permanent self that causes attachment and craving – it is these that lead to dukkha. Buddhism does not reject the Relative Truth of the concept of 'being' – of course we all exist – but as a statement of Ultimate Truth we have no 'self' and are merely a number of aggregates and mental formations dependent for their continuity on many other factors. These aggregates fall into five groups (Pali: khanda): matter (or form), sensations, perceptions, mental functions and consciousness.

The Four States of Consciousness

There are four qualities or States of Consciousness that the Buddha taught should be cultivated. These qualities are often used as meditation subjects. In Pali they are **metta** (loving-kindness, or universal good will), **karuna** (compassion), **mudita** (sympathetic joy) and **upekkha** (equanimity).

Metta is not just the development of warmth or love towards those people that we like, or who have what we personally think of as attractive qualities. It is the cultivation of the wish that <u>all</u> living beings should be happy and free of suffering, and that oneself should be free of enmity and hatred.

Karuna is the compassionate understanding of the plight and suffering of other living beings. It is not the same as sympathy or grief, but is a positive willingness and genuine desire to help others who may be in distress.

Mudita is genuine and spontaneous joy at others' success or happiness. The development of mudita overcomes feelings of envy and jealousy.

Upekkha is the ability to keep a composed mind in those situations when it is not possible to do or say anything constructive. It is not indifference. Upekkha enables one to meet difficult situations without increasing the difficulty through anxiety or useless activity. The development of upekkha through meditation also greatly decreases our senseless worrying about matters over which we have no control.

Kamma*

The Buddha said: "*All beings are the owners of their kamma,*

* *Kamma is the Pali word; the Sanskrit word is Karma.*

*heirs of the kamma, born of their kamma, related to their kamma,
supported by their kamma."*

Kamma is <u>intentional</u> action, through body, speech or mind.
It is both a natural law and a force. It is not the *result* of action,
but only the action itself. Kamma may be good (wholesome) or
bad (unwholesome) to varying degrees, or neutral. The result of
that kamma will be good, bad or neutral accordingly. This is the
Law of Cause and Effect, of action and reaction.

Examples of bodily kamma would include killing and
stealing, or being helpful in practical ways to other people.
Verbal kamma would include lying, gossiping, using abusive
speech to others, or telling the truth.

Mental kamma (always the forerunner to bodily and
verbal kamma) would include trying to improve the mind –
by studying Dhamma or practising meditation, for
example – and by not allowing bad or unwholesome
thoughts to arise in the mind but instead to cultivate good
or wholesome thoughts.

Kamma is an impersonal law that operates independently
of any mysterious outside force, supreme being or ruling
agency. The Buddha taught that a man "reaps what he sows"
– our present situation is the result of past intentional actions
and our future situation will be the result of our present
intentional actions. But within the law of kamma each
person retains free will. We are not merely prisoners of our
past actions.

According to some Buddhist scholars, kammic actions
do not necessarily bring results of the same magnitude. The
results of kamma may be strengthened or weakened by many

variable factors, both at the time the kammic action is performed, and later.

Externally, since our kamma is interwoven with the kamma of all other beings, the conditions for the ripening of an individual's kamma may not arise immediately, or may be modified by external factors.

Internally, the virtuous qualities of an individual's mind may also be sufficient to modify an unwholesome kamma. As an analogy, if a lump of mud is dropped into a small bowl of clear water, the water will become immediately and noticeably dirty. The same lump of mud dropped into a large, clear pool will have considerably less effect. The present mind is, or can be, stronger than the effect of past kamma. Development of good qualities and performance of good deeds in the present can at least partly offset the results of past kamma.

Buddhism also accepts a number of other natural laws that affect our present situation and does not claim that everything is due to past kamma.

The Buddha said: *"All kamma, whether wholesome or unwholesome, will bear fruit. There is no kamma, no matter how insignificant, which is without fruit. As long as an evil deed is not yet ripened, the evil one may perceive his deed as sweet as honey. But when it ripens he will come to grief."*

Some kammas may bring immediate and obvious results. Sometimes the result may come much later, to the extent that the connection between action and result may not be recognisable.

Even many non-Buddhists can probably accept the logic of kamma to an extent, but some have understandably great difficulty with the idea that the result of present kamma may not be in this lifetime, but in a succeeding one.

Rebirth

Rebirth (more properly, re-becoming or re-arising) is not the same as reincarnation. The latter term implies some permanent soul or self that remains constant and unchanging after the death of the physical body, and which transmigrates on death to a new physical body. This is the Eternalist view that Buddhism rejects entirely.

Buddhists believe that in the present moment, thoughts are coming into being and passing away with tremendous speed. As each one ceases, so a new one arises. This causal continuity, the endless arising of moment-to-moment consciousness, operates without the presence of a self, or soul. It is a constant change of mental energies. Each new thought-moment causes change; each is a new birth, conditioned by the previous thought-moment and conditioning the next in an endless chain. As a result of this constant change, we are 'born' and 'die' millions of times in a single physical life-span. If what we think of as 'life' continues without the presence of a permanent self or soul it is reasonable (to Buddhists) that these mental energies must continue up to, and a moment beyond, the cessation of the physical functions, with the last thought-moment of one physical life conditioning the first thought-moment of the re-becoming. As long as there is a clinging to life, a 'will to live' – desire, craving, thirst for existence – the mental energies will seek an immediate rebirth.

Rebirth is a complex and controversial issue, even amongst Buddhist scholars. Some claim that rebirth into a new body immediately follows the death of the last physical body; others that there may be a temporary rebirth in various heavenly realms, or hell states. Some claim that once born into the human realm, it is not possible to be reborn as an animal; others claim that excessive unwholesome kamma may result in rebirth in the animal or lower worlds. Such speculation is really beyond the scope of this beginners' meditation manual. The other aspects of the Buddha's teaching which have been briefly outlined can be proved for oneself through one's own meditation and developing Insight-Wisdom; they are not subject to pointless speculation.

Rebirth, however, will always remain a matter of opinion and conjecture for all but those who achieve Supreme Enlightenment. The Buddha himself said that we should not waste our time pointlessly speculating about what cannot be proved for ourselves, and often refused to answer questions of a speculative nature. Conjecture and opinion may be fine as intellectual entertainment, or for stimulating discussion, but at the end of the day the speculators will be no nearer to knowing the truth for themselves. Whether there is, or is not, rebirth is not an important issue of our lives in the <u>here and now</u> and should not be a factor in the way we conduct ourselves.

We should strive to do good, avoid evil and purify the mind not as an insurance against any possible future life, or to enable us to reach some heavenly sanctuary at the end of this life, but because moral behaviour is conducive to peace, happiness, freedom and, ultimately, Insight.

The Buddha's meditation teaching

The Buddha's main meditation teaching is contained in a discourse called 'The Maha Satipatthana Sutta' – **'The Four Foundations of Mindfulness'**.

The Buddha said of this teaching: *"This is the only way for the purification of beings, for the overcoming of sorrow and lamentation, for the destruction of suffering and grief, for reaching the right path, for the Realisation of Nibbana."*

The discourse is divided into four parts (the Four Foundations):

1. **Contemplation of the body:** including mindfulness of breathing and bodily postures, full attention to physical activities, the internal physical make-up of the body, the material elements of the body, and the impermanence of the body. These should all be observed and known.

2. **Contemplation of feelings:** all feelings, pleasant, unpleasant and neutral, and how they arise and pass away, should be observed and known.

3. **Contemplation of the mind** (or states of consciousness): the states felt by the mind should be observed and known, including lust, hatred, delusion, ignorance, distraction, the 'small' mind, the undeveloped mind, the concentrated mind etc. How such states arise and pass away should be observed and known.

4. **Contemplation of mental objects:** this foundation is concerned with ethical and intellectual subjects, including the hindrances to mental development and spiritual progress, the factors which contribute directly towards Enlightenment, the factors which make up a 'being, the external and internal sense bases, the Four Noble Truths and the Noble Eightfold Path.

The Maha Satipatthana Sutta

A few months after the Buddha's parinirvana his disciples met to classify and authenticate his teachings. The teachings were memorised under different classifications by various groups of senior monks who were responsible for ensuring that the teachings were passed on to succeeding generations of monks without alteration. The oral teachings contained many repetitions to make memorisation easier. The teachings were committed to writing at the earliest 300-400 years after the Buddha's parinirvana and the written teachings contain all the repetitions, which can make reading the texts arduous. Below is a summary of the Maha Satipatthana Sutta, but the list of further suggested reading at the end of this manual includes some books which give a full rendering.

The Buddha was speaking to his monks when he gave this sermon, or discourse, but the teaching applies equally to all meditators.

The Buddha was staying with the Kuru people in the market town of Kammasadhamma when he gathered his monks together and addressed them. He told them that, having overcome feelings of both covetousness and repugnance towards the world, they should clearly and mindfully contemplate the body, feelings, the mind and mental objects.

Contemplation of the body

The Buddha explained how to contemplate the body. He said that the monk should go into a forest, or to some other quiet place, and sit in the meditative posture with the legs crossed and the body erect. The monk should be fully aware (mindful) whilst watching the body breathing in and breathing out, fixing his attention on the act of breathing and knowing whether he is breathing deeply or shallowly, or taking long or short breaths. He should watch with bare awareness as phenomena arise and pass away in the body and mind, whilst not attaching to those phenomena: "clinging to nothing in the world."

The Buddha taught that the monk should be fully and constantly aware of his bodily postures, whether walking, standing, sitting or lying down. Whilst aware of these postures he should watch as phenomena arise and pass away, without attachment.

The monk should pay full attention to, and clearly comprehend, each movement or activity of his body, whether it be walking forward or backward, standing, bending, stretching, wearing the robes, carrying the alms bowl, eating, drinking, chewing, tasting, urinating, defecating, falling asleep, waking, speaking or being silent. In all these activities the monk should be fully aware, knowing that "there is only the body."

The monk should also contemplate the make-up of the physical body. He should be aware that it is composed only of various organs and secretions: hairs of the head, hairs of the body, nails, teeth, skin, flesh, sinews, bones, marrow, kidneys, heart, liver, pleura, spleen, lungs, intestines, mesentery, stomach, excrement, bile, phlegm, pus, blood, sweat, fat, tears, serum, saliva, mucus, synovial fluid and urine. There should be no attachment to the body.*

The monk should also reflect on the body as being composed only of the four primary elements of earth (hardness), water (fluids), fire (heat) and wind (motion).

The monk should be aware of the impermanence of the body by contemplating corpses in charnel grounds. Corpses left for a few days become "swollen, ugly, blue and festering". The corpse may be eaten by crows, vultures, hawks, dogs, jackals and various kinds of small creatures. The corpse eventually becomes a skeleton, "held together by the sinews and with some flesh and blood attached." Finally, all the flesh will be gone, rotted or eaten, until only the skeleton remains. The skeleton will then collapse, reduced to loose scattered bones. Eventually, even the individual bones will bleach and crumble to powder. The monk should contemplate this, and know that his own body is of the same nature and cannot transcend this condition.

---

* Many translations of the Sutta describe this section as contemplation of the 'repulsiveness' of the body, or the 'disgustingness' of the body, or something similar. According to the Pali Text Society in England, such words do not appear in the original text, in which the Buddha said that the body should be viewed just as it is, as a collection of various organs and secretions.

Contemplation of feelings

The Buddha told his monks how to contemplate feelings. When a pleasant feeling arises, the monk should understand that it is just a feeling and that it arises and passes away, and that he should not attach to it. Similarly with feelings that are painful, or neutral, sensual or spiritual. They all merely arise and pass away. The monk should remain completely detached from these feelings, "clinging to nothing in the world".

Contemplation of the mind

Similarly, the monk should know the state of his mind at any time; whether it is lustful, or without lust, hate-filled or without hate, deluded or delusion-free. The monk should know when his mind is in a contracted (small) state, developed, undeveloped, surpassable, unsurpassable, concentrated, unconcentrated, and whether it is a liberated or unliberated state of mind. The monk should contemplate the arising and passing away of these states, knowing, "there is only this, the mind". And he lives without attachment to those states.

Contemplation of mental objects

The monk should contemplate mental objects: the five hindrances to development (sensual desire, ill-will, torpor, restlessness and worry, and doubt); the five aggregates of clinging (material form, feeling, perception, mental formations and consciousness); the six internal and external sense-bases (eye and visual forms, ear and sounds, nose and smells, tongue and tastes, body and tactile impressions, mind and mental objects). With all these internal and external sense-bases, the monk should be aware of the fetter that arises because of their interaction, and he should be aware of how the arisen fetter disappears. The monk contemplates these phenomena without attachment.

The monk should observe and contemplate the Seven Enlightenment Factors as mental objects. When the factor of mindfulness is present, or absent, the monk knows. He knows how this factor arises and how it can be developed and perfected. Similarly with the other Enlightenment factors: investigation of mental objects, energy (self-effort), joy, tranquility, meditative concentration, and equanimity.

The monk should contemplate the Four Noble Truths as mental objects. He should clearly know: "This is dukkha" as reality; he should clearly know: "This is the origin of dukkha" and "This is the cessation of dukkha" and that: "This is the Path leading to the cessation of dukkha."

"This is the only way, monks, for the purification of beings... "

3

Mental development

The modern popular concept of 'meditation' has become far removed from its original meaning: mental development or mental culture (Pali: bhavana). If people think they know anything at all about meditation, they will often believe it means sitting cross-legged, breathing deeply, and having a good think about this or that, which isn't meditation in its original sense at all. Others may believe that meditation is about making the mind blank; of finding a temporary escape from the trials and rigours of daily life – again a mistaken belief, because in true meditation or mental development the mind is constantly 'awake' and aware of everything that is happening within itself and within the body. Through meditation, the mind can be trained to become 'still', and can experience profound peace, but that isn't the same as 'blank'.

The late Phra Acharn Chah, one of Thailand's most influential Dhamma masters and greatly revered by many Western Buddhists, said that the meditator should: *"Try to be mindful and let things take their natural course. Then the mind will become still in any surroundings, like a clear forest pool. All kinds of wonderful, rare animals will come to drink at the pool, and you will clearly see the nature of all things. You will see many strange and wonderful things come and go, but you will be still. This is the happiness of the Buddha".* *

In Buddhism, the mind is the most important element of our make-up and is considered to be another faculty, like the faculty of seeing or hearing. Through the faculties of eye, ear, nose, tongue and body (touch), we are aware of the physical or 'outer world'. With the faculty of mind we experience the 'inner world'; the world of thoughts and ideas, concepts and judgements, cravings, aversions and attachments. The faculty of mind responds to sensory stimuli received by the other faculties. Its present response to those stimuli is usually conditioned by past sensory stimuli and by the demands of what we have come to recognise as our 'self', or ego. The mind's response to external stimuli is usually positive or negative to some degree, but may also be neutral.

Meditation instructors sometimes compare the mind to a mirror. In its original state the mirror is bright and clean, reflecting exactly whatever passes before it. If the mirror is not kept clean and polished, its surface soon becomes covered with a film of dust and dirt, and the images it reflects are no longer clear or true. The images

---

* *From 'A still forest pool', edited by Jack Cornfield and Paul Breitner. Quest Books. 1976.*

become hazy and distorted, until eventually the mirror serves little useful purpose.

The purity of our minds has similarly become defiled by the dirt and dust of years. In the undeveloped mind are all the accumulated hindrances to clear sight, true freedom and happiness: our selfish lusts and hatreds, passions, concepts, envy, greed, conceit, indolence, worry, and delusions of the true nature of the world, and hence of ourselves. The mirror of the mind is completely distorted by these defilements and by the manipulations and demands of the ego. It no longer reflects what is truly there.

The Buddha taught that 'mind' is the forerunner of all intentional actions, including speech. All intentional actions, whether wholesome (Pali: kusala, also translated as positive, good, skillful and wise) or unwholesome (Pali: akusala – negative, bad, unskillful, unwise) are the results of the processes of the mind.

In simple terms, when we use the physical faculties of eye, ear, nose, tongue and body, the nerves and specialised receptor cells of each organ receive the stimulus, then interact with nerve fibres that convey impulses to the central nervous system in the brain. For example, a sight (the stimulus of visible light waves) is received by the receptor (the eye) and is perceived by the brain. Providing the stimulus is not harmful to the receptor, the brain's perception is neutral. The brain may recognise 'light' and no action is necessary, but if a very bright light is perceived the eyes will be instantly closed until the danger to the receptors has passed. The brain also perceives the presence of colour in the light, but doesn't add, *"that's a pretty colour"*.

The brain does not perceive any stimuli as being pleasant or unpleasant, good or bad, desirable or undesirable etc – the mind overlays the neutral perception of the brain with such labels. A sound, for example, is just that, and nothing more, whether it be the Vienna Boys' Choir or a car backfiring. The sound itself carries no emotion, no reaction, no positive or negative feelings; these are the reactions of the mind to the sound. Nothing is intrinsically 'pleasant' or 'unpleasant', 'beautiful', 'ugly', 'desirable', 'good', 'bad' or anything else. These are dualistic conventions, personal concepts, Relative Truths. Everything is just the way it is, but from birth our minds have developed the habit of attaching emotive labels to our sensory perceptions and we react accordingly. Our reactions may be neutral, but more usually will be positive or negative, and may range from very mild to extreme. But whether positive or negative, wholesome or unwholesome, they are frequently of the 'knee-jerk' kind – unconsidered, automatic and conditioned. They may frequently lead to equally unconsidered, automatic, conditioned, unwise or even foolish physical or verbal response. Who hasn't said something without sufficient thought and then instantly regretted it? An *"I could have bitten my tongue off"* type of foolish verbal response. What was said was an unconsidered or unwholesome response and the speaker and others may instantly regret it. They 'suffer'.

Different people's responses to exactly the same stimuli or situations may vary greatly, depending on the past conditioning of their minds. As an example of a mild response to a visual stimulus, you and I may look at a flower – a red rose. If our eyes are comparatively healthy they receive the same light waves.

Exactly the same nerve impulses are sent to your brain and to mine. Our brains translate the impulses and each perceives the form and colour which identifies the thing we call 'a red rose'. The brain of each of us perceives exactly the same thing. But then instantly, your conditioned mind may overlay that clear and neutral perception and say, "I like roses. I like red. I like this flower. It's beautiful. I want it". Mine however, might instantly say, "I don't like roses. I like daffodils. I like yellow. I don't like this flower. It's ugly. Get rid of it". You have a mild degree of craving for it, I have a mild degree of aversion to it.

It is, of course, quite harmless for you to think the rose is beautiful and for me to have the opposite view. In such shallow matters, our different responses wouldn't normally cause any problems, either for ourselves or others. Unless your conditioned craving or my conditioned aversion is more extreme, leading to unwholesome bodily or verbal response, nobody suffers in any sense. We all use such relative, conventional, and personal truths all the time for daily communication: 'an exciting movie', 'an ugly man', 'a beautiful girl', 'a delicious meal', 'a boring book', and so on.

We may have only a very slight dislike or mild aversion for some things, people or situations, but that is just one end of a scale that may culminate in extreme aversion, or even hatred. And even a slight preference for, or clinging to, some thing, person or situation can be continued to the end of a scale that may culminate in a greedy and destructive lust or craving to possess that thing, person, or to be part of that situation. When our conditioned minds start attaching labels of greater intensity to the various phenomena with which we come into contact, and the various stimuli perceived by the brain, and when our craving or aversion become more extreme, then we are more likely to act in unwise or unwholesome ways. The results may be serious and far-reaching, causing mental or physical suffering not only for ourselves, but for others also.

We can, for example, feel slight aversion, intense dislike or even hatred for a particular person just because the neutral physical image perceived by the brain is overlaid and obscured by the conditioned mind with acquired preferences about what constitutes a 'likeable' or 'nice' type of person, and what doesn't. Often we don't even have to know the person as an individual – our minds tell us that we don't like that sort at all. In fact, the person may be entirely free of the negative qualities that our minds apply to him or her. Our aversion may be so strong that we crave to be away from that person, and this may be apparent in our physical and verbal responses. Our minds may even apply such aversion to whole groups, nations or races of people. "I don't like Americans ... blacks ... homosexuals ... Jews ... Communists ... men with beards ... etc etc". The object of our aversion may be completely unaware of our feelings – in which case the suffering is entirely our own.

At their extreme, such unwholesome conditioning harboured in the mind can consume and blind us to all reason. There have, for example, been many incidences of violence, even death, at European football grounds simply because one group supported or liked one team, while another group preferred the opposing team. Each group felt clinging and attachment for their own team and its supporters, and aversion for the rival team and its supporters. The violence that sometimes follows surely indicates minds entirely out of control – in fact it is often referred to as 'mindless violence'.

It could be claimed that such behaviour doesn't stem from hatred or aversion, but from an *enjoyment* in violent and anti-social behaviour. It makes no difference; it all stems from deluded, conditioned and undeveloped minds in which clinging, craving and aversion have reached an extreme level. Wars between entire nations sometimes start for much the same reason; one nation clings to one particular ideology and another to an opposing ideology.

It has become quite common to read of incidences of 'road rage', when drivers use their vehicles as weapons against others to rid themselves of their frustration, anger and impatience – their personal suffering. Many years ago, before the term 'road rage' became popular, I witnessed such an event in London when a car driver, waiting at traffic lights, became impatient (*suffering*) with the driver in front because he didn't move off when the lights changed to green. He tooted his horn. The driver of the car in front got out, dragged the other driver from his car and beat him to death. At the trial later the assailant was said to be an ordinary family man – a 'nice' man – with no history of violent behaviour, but he was under pressure (he was *suffering*) both at home and in his work. The assailant stated later: *"I can't believe I did it"*. His mental suffering had caused him to temporarily lose control of his mind and his ability to respond wisely at the level required by the situation.

Even what is usually considered a 'positive' emotion, like love for another person, when taken to extremes, can delude us. It can cause us to act or react physically and verbally in unwise and ill-considered ways, our reactions dependent on the extent of our clinging or craving, our selfish desires, our envy. 'Love is blind', as the saying goes – sometimes blinded by conditioning to common sense, reason and wisdom.

Of course, that is not to say that we should not love, or form close personal attachments, in either the shallowest or deepest meaning of the word. But, by blindly <u>deluding</u> ourselves in love, by deluding ourselves about the depth and permanence of happiness we believe love can bring, and by foolishly craving for those depths, we must eventually suffer.

"Yes", you might say, "but *I'm* not like that. *I* have more control than that". Perhaps you have, but perhaps you only think you have. You may *think* your mind doesn't respond with conditioned 'knee-jerk' reactions caused by craving or aversion, but it usually does to some degree.

Have you never found yourself in a situation which first made you impatient, then irritable, then angry – progressive stages of the same unwholesome response, and not far removed from *extreme* anger, even violence? Up to what point in that chain of reaction does one remain in control of one's own mind, and hence of one's verbal and physical responses? At what point do such situations get out of hand?

Often our physical and verbal responses are so habitual, so automatic, so conditioned, that we don't even notice them any more, much less wisely consider them. They have become the outward projection of our 'personality', or ego – that which we think of as 'I', 'me', or 'self'. If our physical and verbal actions and reactions are acceptable within our own particular social group or culture, then we take them as being normal and don't stop to think about them. But even 'normal' people can react in extraordinary and socially unacceptable ways – 'out of character' – in some mundane situations if their degree of suffering at a particular moment causes the mind to lose control and become unbalanced.

Of course, most people don't react to their own mental pressures and suffering by 'taking it out on others' in extreme ways, but the undeveloped mind is devious and they may do so in more subtle ways, perhaps even unknown to themselves. An argument at home may make the boss irritable (*suffering*) and he may take his mood out on his staff, finding petty faults in everything they do. Everybody may suffer as a result. Those in a position to assist others may be deliberately or subconsciously uncooperative, determined to cause as much inconvenience as possible.

Even in everyday, mundane situations, when things don't go exactly as *we* think they should, we can react in ridiculously ill-considered or unwholesome ways. Shout at the kids, slam a door, kick the cat, or find some other way to try to relieve our frustration, anger, ill-will, or whatever. All outward expressions of inner mental turmoil and unhappiness – *suffering*. Frequently, we may not even be aware that we are reacting in such physically or verbally unwholesome ways, and when we *are* aware of it, but still continue, we only increase our own suffering.

Instead of taking our mental conflict and suffering out on others, we may take it out on ourselves, perhaps by becoming sulky, or withdrawn, but in extreme cases with sometimes enormously destructive results. Those who commit suicide are often very ordinary people who found themselves in what seemed to be intolerable situations and temporarily lost control; became unbalanced by their own suffering, unbalanced by their aversion to a situation and their craving to escape from it.

It may seem that some of these examples of unwholesome response caused by craving and aversion are extreme, and of course they are. Most people are not football hooligans, murderers, or potential suicides. The fact remains, though, that the hindrances to wise thought and wise response – the past conditioning of our minds and the demands of the ego – make most of us capable of responding to some phenomena or situations to an excessive and unwholesome degree.

The balance of the undeveloped mind is often a fragile balance and can easily become *un*balanced. All the hindrances, prejudices, concepts and delusion are already there, just waiting for the opportunity to spring some surprise, some *"I can't believe I said it"* or *"I can't believe I did it"* type of surprise.

All phenomena, all people, things and situations, with which we come into contact through the five physical faculties cause some level of reaction from the untrained, undeveloped sixth faculty, the mind. We suffer aversion of various degrees to things, people and situations which our minds habitually tell us we don't like, don't want, find ugly, undesirable, unpleasant, unacceptable etc, and suffer accordingly. We crave at various degrees for release from them – and again suffer accordingly.

Equally, we crave for and cling to things, people and situations that our minds are conditioned to believe are desirable, enjoyable or pleasant. When we have them, we cling to them, and when we can't get them, or get them and then lose them, we frequently suffer. Even clinging to, or craving for, the things that make us happy will eventually bring suffering of one kind or another to the untrained, undeveloped mind.

Your beautiful red rose will wither and die. Although your 'suffering' from clinging to the rose is not likely to send you into paroxysms of grief; if we change the example of the rose to a beloved *person* – and as people we all share the same eventual fate as the flower – at the other end of the scale the degree of self-induced suffering can become extreme. Simply because we are not able to accept the ultimate impermanence and 'unsatisfactoriness' of all phenomena at anything but the most superficial level.

<u>Nothing</u> remains the same for two consecutive moments. All physical and mental phenomena are in a state of constant flux, but the undeveloped mind continues to crave for them, cling to them, or suffer aversion to them, attaching concepts to them as though they were permanent and unchanging. And suffering of one degree or another must inevitably result. But the mind freed through mental development from its attachments, craving, aversion and delusion, freed of its personal concepts and prejudices of all kinds, freed of the illusion of 'I' and 'self', is a balanced and healthy mind, a totally *clean* mind, a pure mind. It operates from a basis of wisdom and sees with clear comprehension, and hence sees the true nature of all phenomena with which it comes into contact.

Although the developed mind does not react with 'knee-jerk' and habitual and conditioned response, this does not mean that we become emotionless, or 'cold'. Far from it. As we develop the mind through meditation, so we increasingly start to react at exactly the <u>right level</u> to any phenomena perceived by the brain, or in which we are involved. We neither under-react, nor over-react. Our reactions are based on wisdom – Insight-Wisdom – and other qualities that are developed through meditation. We live in peace and harmony with ourselves, with others, and with our environment.

It is to achieve that end that the Buddha taught his meditation techniques. To rid the mind of the defilements, hindrances and impurities that prevent the arising of Insight-Wisdom.

Meditation in its true Buddhist sense is not an easy undertaking. To achieve anything other than the most superficial results and benefits requires enormous commitment, effort, diligence and patience. At first there may be little of these qualities in the beginner, but even a little can 'get the ball rolling', and as practice progresses so these qualities also increase. Their natural and progressive development is one of the benefits of meditation.

There are two techniques of meditation practised by Buddhist meditators: **Samatha** and **Vipassana.**

Samatha

Samatha is Concentration or Calmness Meditation. It helps develop **one-pointedness of mind.** (Pali: cittekaggata).

The practice of Samatha can lead to very intense, trance-like 'Absorbtion States', in which the consciousness gradually transcends everyday reality to other levels or 'spheres'. In these trance-like states the hindrances and impurities of the mind may seem to disappear, and the meditator may be deluded into sensations of great tranquility and happiness. In fact, the hindrances are merely suppressed, not eradicated, and Samatha does not lead to the arising of Insight-Wisdom. Except at the very lowest levels, the spheres are said to be difficult to attain. In this manual, Samatha meditation is practised only as an aid to Vipassana, and to increase concentration ability.

Samatha was known and practised in India centuries before the Buddha's lifetime. The Buddha – as the ascetic Gotama – studied and practised Samatha with the greatest yogic teachers of the time. But despite his total proficiency, he realised that Samatha could not lead to Enlightenment, the arising of Insight-Wisdom, since the various spheres were themselves mind-produced, conceptual and therefore delusory.

In his final great effort to reach Enlightenment, the ascetic Gotama passed beyond the conceptual Absorbtion States of Samatha, to a new level of understanding; to the realisation of all things as Ultimate Truth. He became Enlightened and henceforth was known as The Buddha. The Buddha's meditation teaching is known as Vipassana and is true Buddhist meditation. It is only this meditation that can lead to purification of the mind, and hence to Nibbana.

Vipassana

Vipassana, or Insight Meditation, uses the concentration built up from Samatha meditation to observe with **bare awareness** the constantly changing phenomena occurring within the practitioner's body and mind.

In Vipassana, the meditator 'opens up' to everything going on in the body and mind without deliberately trying to exclude or suppress any physical sensation, emotion or thought that arises, whether wholesome or unwholesome, pleasant or unpleasant, subtle or intense. All are simply observed, recognised and acknowledged as they arise and pass away. The meditator tries not to feel either aversion or attachment for them, but simply watches dispassionately and objectively with bare awareness. Whilst the meditator does not try to suppress the various phenomena, they are not dwelt upon or allowed to lead to discursive or judgmental thinking. Neither the past nor the future have any reality and the mind exists with just bare awareness only in the present moment, the here and now. It merely observes with equanimity.

This is not self analysis, but rather *no-self* analysis, for as we observe the ever-changing mental phenomena we can see that there is nothing permanent in them, nothing with which we can identify as being 'I', 'me' or 'mine'. We begin to have a clearer understanding of our own reality, and to see from where and how our delusion and suffering arise. We also see that the physical body and its various sensations are constantly changing, and that there is nothing within it with which we can identify, nor to which we can attach. It is temporarily ours, not 'I', 'me' or 'mine', but rather something borrowed from the earth, which cannot belong to us, and over which we have little control.

We begin to recognise the mind's impurities, to see why they exist and why they arise; and by not attaching to them in any way it becomes gradually easier to let them go. As our meditation skill develops, we can go further, to the sometimes very deep roots of the impurities and defilements, and eliminate them. The layers of prejudices and preferences, cravings and aversions, lustful desires, greed, ill-will, jealousy, conceit, worry, and delusion that have built up in the mind from the moment of birth are gradually cleansed from the mind. The mirror of the mind once again reflects without distortion.

At the same time as the impurities and defilements are overcome, so their opposites are developed – greater concentration, greater awareness, increased mental energy and will-power, greater confidence and tranquility.

The realisations that arise as a result of the dispassionate observation of physical and mental phenomena are the beginnings of Insight-Wisdom. But this Insight-Wisdom cannot be obtained by intellectual investigation – it can <u>only</u> arise intuitively. It must be self-realised.

Insight-Wisdom may not arise in a sudden flash all at once. There are many truths, many insights to be realised along the way. For most people it takes time, very great patience and perseverance. The meditator must not expect 'results' every time he or she sits down to practise. To *expect* anything in meditation, to want, desire, or crave for results, defeats the entire purpose of the practice, which is the elimination of craving.

The benefits of meditation

Even if the practitioner does not achieve the ultimate 'goal', meditation can bring many benefits to daily life. People progress and develop at different rates in their meditation, so it is impossible to forecast that an individual will start to see or feel benefits in some specific time. Only one thing is certain – persevere and you *will* progress, you *will* benefit. Progress does not necessarily mean practising the more complex exercises in this manual for hours on end. Even the simplest exercises, if practised with complete mindfulness, can bring about the fullest benefits.

The earliest benefits to become apparent for most people are likely to be fairly superficial. For example, even a short time spent in sitting meditation can calm and relax body and mind long after the practice is over. Deeper and more relaxed sleep usually follows lying meditation and the overall physical and mental health can improve as a result. Many meditators claim that stress-related illnesses such as high blood pressure and ulcers can show great improvement; muscle tensions and headaches can be relieved and depression and anxiety lifted.

Concentration ability and energy levels can rise significantly, bringing benefits in everyday life in the home, at work or at school, and in the social environment.

Gradually an increased ability to cope with day-to-day problems will become apparent – the ability to face the hassles of life with greater control and equanimity. Unhappiness at what were perceived to be 'impossible' situations may no longer arise. Problems that previously seemed insurmountable will be seen in quite a different way, and can be tackled with a more positive and more efficient attitude. Perhaps they will no longer be seen as problems at all.

During meditation we constantly and dispassionately observe thoughts, ideas, concepts and emotions that arise in the mind, and train ourselves to 'let them go'; not to attach to them or consider them as 'belonging' to us. So there is increasingly less concept of 'I' or 'self' and the habitual egotistic cravings, aversions and fixed views which always attend these illusory ideas. We learn to remain aloof from them, unattached and unaffected by them. Our personal preferences become less defined, less automatic, less biased. We begin to evaluate all phenomena from a basis of clear wisdom, rather than with our conditioned and habitual ideas. At the same time, we also cultivate other qualities: compassion for others, equanimity, joy and goodwill.

These skills, or new ways of looking at life, are an indication of a gradually developing wisdom, an understanding of one's own mind and the way things *are* that comes directly from meditation practice.

It may be a long process, for many people have years of delusion and conditioning to overcome, but eventually an inner peace will develop in the mind, and the mind can remain still in any situation, simply accepting what *is*.

The meditation system described in this manual comes directly from that taught by the Buddha. The system is taught by most of the meditation masters of Thailand, Myanmar (Burma), Sri Lanka and other Asian countries, and by many meditation centres in the West.

4

The key to concentration

An important aid for beginners in meditation is the use of mental acknowledgements. These are words, or groups of words, 'spoken' in the mind. They help to keep the concentration anchored on a single object or activity, bring it back when it has wandered, and help the practitioner dispassionately identify and then let go of various feelings or phenomena that arise in the body and mind.

Everybody can concentrate to a degree, especially when doing something that holds the interest. It is relatively easy to concentrate on a good book, or an exciting movie, or when trying to solve a difficult problem. But even when we are doing something which we personally find interesting, the mind is easily distracted and we cannot keep our *full* attention on anything for more than a few seconds at a time. Some psychologists claim that the attention span of the average, undeveloped mind is only about 3.5 seconds.

All beginners in meditation are constantly distracted, particularly by random thoughts that arise in the mind. These random thoughts can lead to day-dreaming or discursive thinking, with a consequent loss of concentration. This can be very frustrating and some new practitioners may very early on begin to develop a sense of failure, to feel it's 'hopeless', and that perhaps meditation is too difficult. These feelings are themselves hindrances to progress and this is the time when the new practitioner needs great patience, diligence and perseverance if any progress is to be made. With perseverance, a measure of control can be established over the mind and concentration levels will increase. Mental acknowledgements help considerably.

In practice, the differences between Samatha and Vipassana can sometimes be quite subtle and it is easy for Vipassana to cross over into Samatha, or vice versa. It should be remembered that although Samatha can increase concentration levels, as well as bringing many other benefits, it alone does not lead to the arising of Insight-Wisdom. Only Vipassana can do that. Although Samatha can be practised on its own for the sake of its own benefits, in this manual it is considered as an aid to Vipassana. A period of Samatha meditation is therefore always practised prior to a period of Vipassana.

One of the purposes of Samatha is to still the mind, to stop it constantly jumping from one apparently random thought to another, and to train it to operate more calmly, more efficiently, and with longer attention spans. When it is able to concentrate on one specific object the mind is said to be 'one-pointed', and the meditator carries out the action with '**mindfulness**'. (Pali: sati). When the meditator carries that mindfulness and concentration over to Vipassana meditation, it becomes a valuable tool.

All meditation needs an object of primary attention, an 'anchor point'; either a physical movement or bodily process, or an abstract idea. Otherwise the mind is quickly drawn into day-dreaming and discursive thinking. Many meditation centres recommend that the breathing process (watching the in and out breaths) should be the primary attention point in Vipassana, but they may also frequently recommend the same primary attention point for Samatha. Some meditation centres combine the principles of Samatha and Vipassana into one discipline. Some centres teach walking meditation to increase concentration, when mindfulness is kept totally on specific movements of the feet; but at the same time they may recommend making mental acknowledgements which are more suitable to Vipassana meditation. This can be quite confusing for the beginner who, in practice, may not be sufficiently experienced to fully differentiate between the two meditation methods.

In this manual there are very specific differences between Samatha and Vipassana meditation. The walking meditation exercises are used only to build up concentration ability as an aid to Vipassana. To do that, the exercises use mental acknowledgements which help keep the mind focussed only on movements of the feet, whilst ignoring all sensory stimuli. The Vipassana sitting meditation makes use of that increased concentration and also uses suitable mental acknowledgements; but their purpose then is to help the meditator recognise <u>everything</u> that is arising in the body and mind, ignoring nothing.

For the beginner practising Samatha, acknowledgement of any distraction to the main activity may actually lead the meditator into becoming more and more involved with the distraction. The untrained mind can then very quickly be sidetracked and concentration may be lost. In Vipassana, <u>all</u> phenomena are an element of the meditation to be observed, but in Samatha the mind must be one-pointed only on the object of meditation at all times.

When practising walking meditation as an aid to Vipassana, anything that distracts the concentration from the present movement of the foot is ignored as much as possible. The meditator is not interested in anything happening within the physical body, within the mind, or which is perceived externally. All external stimuli – anything seen, heard, smelt, tasted or touched – are ignored. Hearing a neighbour's dog barking, for example, will distract from the object of concentration, just as it would if one was absorbed in a good book. All internal sensations, whether they be physical aches and pains, or thoughts and emotions that come into the mind, are ignored. Remembering some incident from the past, or thinking about something that needs to be done in the future, are distractions to be ignored. When using walking meditation as an aid to Vipassana we don't think about <u>anything</u> except the object of concentration; the mindfulness is only on the activity of the moment. During walking meditation, the practitioner should not try to put a name to the distractions or acknowledge them in any way.

In Vipassana, rather than concentrating exclusively on one object to the exclusion of all else, we instead 'open up' to everything going on in the body and mind; to outside stimuli, to physical sensations as they arise and pass away, and to mental formations as they arise and pass away. What in Samatha are distractions to be ignored become an important element of Vipassana meditation. In Vipassana, the barking dog causes 'hearing' to arise, and if the barking continues, there may arise sensations of irritation, ill-will, or even anger towards the dog or its owner, so the sound and the mind's reaction to it become part of the overall meditation.

Although in Vipassana we are aware of everything going on within the body and mind, we still need a primary attention point, or anchor point, to which we can return between observation of other phenomena. We need a place of attention from where we can observe the various physical and mental phenomena objectively, without any sense of 'I' being involved. For this we use the in and out breaths. The breath is emotionally neutral; we do it all the time and, if we are breathing normally, it is not something we attach to or need to be 'personally' involved with.

Although using the in and out breaths as an anchor point, the breathing process itself is also part of the Vipassana meditation object, which is <u>all</u> the various processes and sensations of the body and mind.

Mental acknowledgements in walking meditation

If it is difficult to concentrate fully on something that we find interesting, it is considerably more so to concentrate fully for any length of time on a simple thing like raising the foot in walking meditation. The movements involved in walking make good objects for concentration because we usually undertake them with little or no conscious thought. It is only when we really try to concentrate totally on them that we realise how little control we have over our own minds.

Walking meditation is taught in six stages. In each stage the simple act of raising and moving the foot forward is broken down into progressively more movements. Each movement made is mentally acknowledged with a word or group of words that describes the movement. For example, when lifting the foot prior to moving it forward, we acknowledge *lifting*. When moving it forward, we acknowledge *moving*. When lowering the foot to the floor, we acknowledge *lowering*. In later exercises the movements are broken down still further.

In addition to acknowledging the movements involved in walking we also acknowledge the turning movements which are made at each end of the walking path. Turning is made in several stages and each stage is acknowledged as *turning*. Before commencing to walk, we spend a few moments being totally mindful of the body in the standing position, acknowledging *standing*. As progress is made through the six stages, we start to acknowledge not only the movements themselves, but also the intention to move. For example, while standing still and immediately before taking the first step on the walking path, we acknowledge *intending to walk.* At the end of each length of the path, before turning, we acknowledge *intending to turn,* before acknowledging the movements made in turning. (The six stages of walking meditation, and the relevant acknowledgements, are described fully in chapter 8.)

It is of great importance that mental acknowledgements must be used very precisely if they are to be of any help. There is no point mentally acknowledging *lifting* if the foot is already moving forward. In that case the acknowledgement would be helping to concentrate the mind on a movement which is already in the past. Similarly, there is no point acknowledging *lowering* if the foot has not yet finished its forward motion – that would be concentrating the mind on a future movement. When in meditation, we exist only in the present moment and are not concerned with what has gone before, nor with what will come after. The mind is one-pointed in the here and now. Acknowledgement of an intention to move <u>must</u> be made before the action is commenced, and cannot overlap into the action. Acknowledgement of the action itself <u>must</u> be made during the course of the action, and neither before nor after.

There is no particular importance in the acknowledgement words themselves and they are <u>not</u> the objects of concentration – they are only aids. When acknowledging any intention or movement it is not enough to simply picture the word, or say it under the breath. The meditator must <u>know</u> the intention or movement. In walking meditation, concentration is always totally on the movement of the foot at any particular moment and the mental acknowledgement of the movement helps anchor the concentration to that focus point.

If practising meditation at a centre, usually as part of a group, the instructor will quite often make the walking meditation acknowledgements aloud for the benefit of the whole group. This can be helpful for the absolute beginner but, since 'hearing' is involved when somebody else is making the acknowledgements, it can reduce the meditator's one-pointedness. It is better to get used to making your own acknowledgements to help you concentrate, even if at first you have to make them 'under the breath'.

Mental acknowledgements in sitting meditation

The mental acknowledgements in Vipassana meditation are *rising* and *falling*, referring to the movements of the abdomen whilst breathing in and out, or *breathing in* and *breathing out* if using the nose tip as an anchor point.

In Vipassana, all physical and mental sensations that momentarily arise and pass away are observed. The breathing process is observed continuously, since that is also an activity of the body. The acknowledgements used to help keep concentration on the breath are extremely important and must be focussed very precisely if the meditation is to progress and develop. It is therefore necessary to know how we breathe in meditation.

Breathing

In Vipassana the primary object of concentration or focusing of awareness is breathing: 'knowing the breaths'. But the breath, or breathing process, may be observed in several different ways and at various points: at the nose, in the rise and fall of the abdomen, or its passage can be traced from the nose, through the body and out again. Different meditation centres teach different anchor points, often depending on the instructor's own training or personal preference. The Vipassana exercises later in this manual use the rise and fall of the abdomen as their anchor point, but it is up to the individual meditator to decide which point is most personally precise, and which method most beneficial.

Manuals or instructors that prefer the nose tip often simply say, "focus your awareness on the in and out breaths at the nose tip", or something similar. However, it is possible to be more precise than that, though how much precision different individuals can achieve depends entirely on the shape of the nose, the shape of the upper lip, and whether the nose overhangs the upper lip.

Many people can find their own most precise anchor point by taking several deep breaths and breathing out sharply through the nose. The point around the area of the nose and upper lip where the passage of expelled air is most obvious will be the point of concentration, even though whilst in meditation the practitioner breathes at a normal speed.

Some people breathe naturally shallowly and for them even a sharp exhalation may not identify the most precise concentration point. Quite often the point of maximum awareness of the breath is on the septal cartilage – the hard flexible wall that separates the nostrils. Although in a clear nose the air enters and leaves through two nostrils, each breath is felt to be entering and leaving through a single cavity. It is on the septal cartilage that it can be most easily identified.

Some people are aware of the air entering the nose as it passes over the septal cartilage and aware of it leaving as it passes over the upper lip. Identify <u>one</u> point at which the passage of air can be felt most obviously and make that the anchor point in all your Vipassana meditation.

If following the rise and fall of the abdomen, the concentration/anchor point is an imagined circle a few inches across and about two inches below the navel. There is no need to mentally visualise an actual circle (though in early practice you can, if it helps); just identify a very localised point whilst sitting in the meditation position you plan to adopt for practice. (Meditation positions are described in chapter 5.)

When observing the movement of the abdomen and acknowledging *rising... falling...* the point of concentration must be on the abdominal cavity and, more precisely, the 'circle' where the movement seems most obvious. When following the rise and fall of the abdomen you should be concerned only with the movement itself, not with the abdomen or the abdominal organs. If concentrating on the rising and falling of the abdomen, ignore the passage of air through the nostrils, and vice versa.

Some meditation centres teach that the passage of air should be observed as it enters the nose, followed through the body as the abdomen rises and falls, and back out again through the nose. Other centres teach that this is not such a good method for the beginner. Meditators who use this method may consciously or unconsciously slow their breathing down and breathe more deeply, so that the whole passage of air may be more easily observed. As a relaxation exercise, or for use in concentration meditation, the method has much to recommend it, but for the beginner it may not be so suitable.

When watching the breath, either at the nose tip or abdomen, it is not necessary to breathe deliberately slowly, deeply, quickly, or shallowly. Allow the body to regulate its own intake of air and don't consciously attempt to alter it. Just let everything take its own course and dispassionately observe. Whether the body is taking a long breath, or a short breath, a fast or slow breath, simply observe it. There may come a time in future practice when the breathing slows down so much that it may be hard to observe at all. This is natural in meditation and is not something to be concerned about. It should be acknowledged in a similarly dispassionate way to all other phenomena.

When in sitting meditation and breathing at a normal pace, each in-breath is mentally acknowledged as *rising*. The mental acknowledgement must be made while the abdomen is being observed to move upwards. People who breathe naturally slowly may need to make the acknowledgement more than once: *rising... rising... rising* to cover the entire motion. Similarly, when breathing out, the acknowledgement *falling* is made and it must cover the entire period of the fall. If focussed on the nose tip, acknowledge *breathing in... breathing out,* making the acknowledgements as many times as necessary to fully cover each stage.

The Vipassana sitting exercises in this manual start off very simply, but later exercises become more complex. In those, between the acknowledgements of the breathing process, the meditator also starts to mentally examine various parts of the body; to momentarily place the awareness in those parts and to observe any sensations that exist or are arising. Some parts of the body come under more physical strain than others during meditation. For example, a knee resting on the floor surface, or the buttocks against the meditation cushion. These physical sensations are dispassionately observed, recognised and acknowledged.

Other physical sensations, such as an ache, or itch, may arise of themselves. They are observed dispassionately and acknowledged as *aching* or *itching* and then concentration is returned to the rise and fall of the abdomen. Often sensations of discomfort will pass after several acknowledgements. When we feel an ache or itch that refuses to subside even after several acknowledgements, and we decide to change position, or scratch, we acknowledge first the intention: *intending to move* and then the movements involved in the change of position or the act of scratching: *aching... aching... intending to move... intending to move... moving... moving... moving... flexing... shifting...* and awareness is returned to the rise and fall of the abdomen.

No matter how hard we try to find the 'ideal' place for sitting meditation there will always be various external stimuli to be acknowledged, as well as the sensations and feelings that arise in the mind as a result of them. A telephone will ring, a dog will bark, a door will slam, we may smell something, we may feel too hot, or too cold. Internally, thoughts, ideas, memories and emotional feelings and sensations may arise.

During Vipassana meditation, when we hear a noise we acknowledge *hearing*. When we smell something, *smelling*. It is important not to become involved in analysis of the stimuli, thinking, for example, "That's the neighbour's horrible dog barking", or "What's that smell?" The mind will be instantly drawn away from the meditation. The acknowledgement of the stimulus should be made, and then full awareness should be returned to the rise and fall of the abdomen. When acknowledging dispassionately in this way, the mind will often cease to be aware of the stimulus, even if it continues.

Mental sensations take many forms but are treated in the same way. When concentration has been lost and, for example, we find ourselves planning something, we recognise the thoughts and acknowledge them: *planning*. If we find ourselves remembering some incident from the past: *remembering*. Sometimes, for no apparent reason and without being preceded by discursive thoughts or day-dreaming, some strong emotion will arise, such as anger or happiness. We simply observe the arising of the emotion, acknowledge it dispassionately, let it go and return to the rise and fall of the abdomen. Even happy thoughts or sensations should not be dwelt upon, but are simply observed with bare awareness. The acknowledgement are not used to suppress these thoughts or emotions, but to help the meditator recognise them as they arise and pass away.

Do not search the mind for suitable acknowledgement words, as that itself may lead to discursive thinking. If you cannot immediately think of something more precise, just acknowledge *thinking*. Whatever is perceived from 'outside', or arises in the mind, and no matter how frequently it occurs, simply dispassionately observe, acknowledge, let it go and return awareness to the rising and falling of the abdomen.

Some suggested acknowledgement words are given at the end of this chapter.

In everyday situations and conversations, we all frequently need to think or refer to ourselves as 'I', 'me', 'my': 'I am hearing', 'I have a pain', 'I am bored', and so on. In meditation we do not think in terms of 'I' at all. We acknowledge *standing,* not *I am standing, hearing* not *I am hearing, bored* not *I am bored, anger* not *my anger.* Whenever we think in terms of 'I', 'me' or 'my', our clear and neutral perception is instantly clouded by conditioning, by our cravings and aversions. These purely subjective preferences are hindrances to the clear perception and acceptance of the way things actually are. One of the goals of the meditator is to clear away these cravings and aversions, prejudices and preferences; to simply observe dispassionately and impersonally. When that is achieved, Insight-Wisdom can arise.

Mental acknowledgements in practice

To give an idea of how mental acknowledgements should be used in practice, here is an example of a couple of minutes of sitting meditation which immediately follows a period of walking meditation.

You are on the final length of your walking path which, in an ideal situation, has brought you to the place where you intend practising sitting meditation.

The eyes are still open from walking meditation. When you reach the sitting place, stand perfectly still for a few moments, acknowledging *standing... standing... standing.* Your whole awareness must be with that position – there is no point acknowledging *standing* while also thinking, *I'm going to sit down next.* The future, even if it is only a moment away, is not the concern <u>now.</u> Now, you are 'standing', and that is your only awareness. Make the acknowledgement *standing* as many times as necessary until you are totally aware of the body in that position.

You are ready to sit and you acknowledge that intention: *intending to sit... intending to sit... intending to sit.* You must not start to sit whilst that acknowledgement is in your mind. You must be aware only of the intention to sit.

The movements and acknowledgements made during changing from the standing position to the sitting position will vary from person to person. The acknowledgements I give are from my own observation of how different meditators move when making the change. I have simplified the movements, and there are other acknowledgements that could be made, but keep your movements and acknowledgements fairly simple in early practice. As your meditation develops and your mindfulness increases, you should be able to break down your movements increasingly further and acknowledge accordingly.

In changing from standing to sitting, you might first bend one leg and lower yourself onto one knee, the right knee, for example. Acknowledge *bending... bending... bending... lowering... lowering... lowering.* At the moment the knee touches the floor, so you may also reach out your right hand and lower it to the ground to support yourself: *touching... touching... touching... reaching... reaching... reaching... lowering... lowering... lowering... touching... touching.* Then, you may lower the rest of the body: *lowering... lowering... lowering* and your left knee will touch the floor: *touching... touching.* You may then fold the right leg underneath the body: *bending... bending... bending* and reach the left hand to the left foot and raise the foot to rest it on the right calf: *reaching... reaching... grasping... grasping... raising... raising... touching.* The hands are then moved slowly to the lap: *moving... moving... moving.* You are now in your meditation position and you acknowledge that for a few moments whilst being fully aware of the body in the sitting position: *sitting... sitting... sitting.*

You may need to fidget around for a few moments whilst making yourself comfortable on the cushion: *fidgeting... fidgeting... fidgeting.* When you are sure you are comfortable, you are ready to start your sitting practice.

Take a couple of deep breaths and then allow the breathing to settle into a normal rhythm. Do not force the abdomen to settle into a rhythm by deliberately breathing faster, slower, deeper or shallower – let the breathing find its own natural level.

The eyes have remained open during the change from standing to sitting, but you now prepare to close them: *intending to close... intending to close... intending to close.* Allow the eyes to close slowly: *closing... closing.*

Focus your attention on the abdominal 'circle': *focussing... focussing... focussing.*

Mentally watch the abdomen rise: *rising... rising.* Watch the abdomen fall: *falling... falling.* The acknowledgements must cover the entire rise and fall. If they don't, do not speed up or slow down the breathing to match the acknowledgements – speed up or slow down the acknowledgements instead. It doesn't matter how many times the acknowledgements need to be made, as long as they cover the entire action. But equally, they must not overlap – you must not still be acknowledging *rising* if the abdomen has started its fall.

For some people, the end of the fall may not be obvious. Do not force the abdomen to fall by squeezing the stomach muscles. Instead, take as the end of the fall the moment when you are no longer aware of obvious movement.

Within seconds the mind will be thoroughly bored with this and some discursive thought will arise: "I'm bored", or "I'm meditating". Dispassionately acknowledge *bored* or *thinking* (not *I am bored* or *I am thinking*), let the feeling or thought go and bring the attention back to the rise and fall. A few seconds later, you will again suddenly realise the attention has wandered and that you are, perhaps, remembering something that happened earlier in the day. Dispassionately observe and acknowledge the thoughts: *remembering... remembering*, let them go and return to the rise and fall.

This 'letting go' of discursive thoughts or emotions that arise is not easy at first. Sometimes the mind follows the path of the thoughts and becomes increasingly more involved and entangled with them. At the point where you realise this has happened, acknowledge: *knowing... knowing*, and drag your awareness back to the rise and fall of the abdomen.

Whatever thoughts arise, dispassionately observe, acknowledge and let them go. You may become frustrated or annoyed with yourself for your lack of concentration and control over your own mind. There is no need to be. Simply acknowledge: *impatient, frustrated* or *annoyed,* or whatever is the strongest emotion, let it go and return to the rise and fall.

Acknowledgements of the rise and fall of the abdomen, of external stimuli, of mental and sensory formations, of intentions and movements, must be <u>continuous.</u> There must be no gaps in your acknowledgements. As soon as you leave an unacknowledged space you will lose control. Many thousands of acknowledgements could be made in just an hour's sitting practice.

It is important that the acknowledgements *rising* and *falling* should not become automatic, like some sort of mantra or chant. The awareness point is <u>not</u> in the words themselves; it must be with the action. The acknowledgements, all acknowledgements, are merely an aid to help you focus the awareness.

Just a minute or so of sitting meditation may take the following course:

Rising... falling... thinking... thinking... distracted... rising... falling... ri..itching... itching...rising... intending to move... intending to move... moving... moving... moving... scratching... scratching... moving... moving... falling... rising... what's on TV tonight? Damn!... thinking... thinking... annoyed... rising... falling...ri..hearing... whose dog is that barking?... Oh dear... falling... rising... this is so boring... bored... bored... impatient... rising... falling... rising...how long have I been sitting so far? Arrgh!... rising... etc.

If you haven't given up already, your alarm clock will ring at the end of the pre-set time: *hearing... ˙hearing... hearing.* Do not immediately get up from the sitting position. Raise the right hand slowly from the lap: *raising... raising* and place it on the right knee: *lowering... lowering...*

touching. Do the same with the left hand, acknowledging the movements as you do so. Slowly open the eyes: *intending to open... opening... opening.*

Be aware that the eyes are now receiving sensory impressions, but do not be immediately concerned or involved in what they are seeing: *seeing... seeing... seeing.* Slowly unfold the legs, acknowledging the intention and each movement: *intending to move... intending to move... moving... moving... moving... unfolding... unfolding... straightening... straightening... rubbing... rubbing... rubbing* etc. Slowly rise to a standing position, acknowledging as many of the movements as you can. Let the arms hang by your sides, acknowledging and being totally aware of the position: *standing... standing... standing.*

Although your formal practice is now finished, you should continue to move slowly and mindfully, whilst acknowledging as many intentions and movements as possible, until you need to start moving at a normal pace again.

Some meditators find that as their practice develops and they become naturally more mindful, the use of so many acknowledgements becomes less necessary. However, the practitioner must not make a conscious decision to stop using them. As mindfulness becomes more firmly established, the acknowledgements may fade away of their own accord, though full awareness will be maintained.

Variations of your main practice

Although this chapter has referred specifically to the use of mental acknowledgements in walking and sitting meditation, the exercises detailed later include mindfulness exercises and Vipassana lying meditation.

Mindfulness exercises are simple, mundane activities which involve and combine a number of different physical movements. These movements, and the intentions, are acknowledged in exactly the same way as you will practise in walking meditation.

Vipassana lying meditation uses a lying-down position, instead of a sitting position, but the primary attention point remains either in the rise and fall of the abdomen, or the in and out breaths at the nose tip.

Suggested acknowledgement words

Some exercises that are described later have standard acknowledgement words, but the following will also be useful for various types of practice. Add others if you want, but keep them as short, precise and as simple as possible. Before you commence practising meditation, become familiar with the acknowledgement words you might use. That way, whilst in meditation the mind will not have to search around for a suitable word for any physical or mental sensation that arises, and hence become further distracted from the meditation itself.

Seeing	Hearing	Smelling
Tasting	Touching	Feeling
Perceiving	Knowing	Itching
Aching	Painful	Throbbing
Hurting	Happy	Bored
Sad	Content	Angry

Irritated	Desiring	Wanting
Dreaming	Doubting	Thinking
Imagining	Remembering	Planning
Wishing	Sleepy	Drowsy
Worrying	Annoyed	Frustrated
Impatient	Comfortable	Uncomfortable
Moving	Raising	Lowering
Stretching	Reaching	Pushing
Pulling	Opening	Closing
Holding	Grasping	Twisting
Scratching	Rubbing	Bending
Placing	Standing	Sitting
Unfolding	Folding	Hot
Cold	Warm	Sweating
Shivering	Moving	Focussing
Turning	Fidgeting	

After undertaking any of the various meditation exercises, it can be a good idea to list the mental acknowledgements you can remember making. Go over all your movements, sensory perceptions and mental formations to see where you could have made acknowledgements but didn't. Add them to your list. However, you should never use a written list during the exercises – that would simply be reading and is of no value at all.

5

Practising the practice

Before attempting any meditation, it is helpful for the beginner to spend some time practising and becoming familiar with the positions and movements involved. Some meditative positions and movements may seem awkward, uncomfortable and distracting at first. If you can train yourself in the practicalities, the meditation itself is more likely to get off to a better and more productive start, and with less to think or worry about. All the movements in meditation should be practised until they can be made slowly, but fluidly. Practising some of the movements in front of a full-length mirror can be helpful. No movements in meditation should be automatic, and as many as possible should be acknowledged, so the beginner will usually have to move much more slowly than usual. As the meditation progresses and mindfulness develops, so some movements will speed up naturally, but without loss of concentration.

Walking meditation

Walking meditation is used to build up concentration ability, which is necessary for the most successful practice of sitting meditation.

When walking under normal circumstances, our movements are almost entirely automatic, requiring little concentration or conscious thought. We often have to be mindful of the surface we are walking on – whether it is loose or irregular, whether it has steps, kerbs or other hazards, whether it is hard or soft, slippery or dry, but all this is necessary awareness of the prevailing conditions. We may adjust our walking speed or style to take account of potential hazards, but in normal conditions the process of moving the feet is likely to be at best semi-automatic. Who hasn't tripped on a raised paving stone, or trodden in something nasty, because they weren't sufficiently concentrating on where they were putting their feet?

Walking meditation is not practised to enable us to walk without tripping over our own feet. It is a meditation training that uses the ordinary act of walking as its object. It concentrates the mind on the individual movements needed to take one step at a time, but that increased concentration ability can be applied to all other activities too.

Concentration levels must be built up gradually. Walking meditation is taught in six progressive stages that combine different movements. One would hardly think that a simple action like moving a foot forward could be so complex, but that is because we usually don't think about it at all. That is the whole point; to make the meditator aware and to concentrate the mind on this simple physical movement, to separate the mental intention of moving from the physical action itself, and to keep the mind concentrated in the present moment.

The various specific movements of each stage of walking meditation are explained in the relevant exercises, but each stage includes periods of standing still, and turning the body at the end of each length of the walking path.

Standing still position

The standing still position is used at the commencement of walking meditation, at the end of each length of the walking path before and after turning, and when changing from walking to sitting meditation. Standing still in meditation isn't just 'standing still'– it is an important meditative posture and can help the practitioner develop very great concentration, as well as an increased awareness and understanding of the physical body.

You may think that when standing straight and still, the body is relaxed. That isn't the case, for even when standing perfectly still the body uses up to about 140 calories per hour. Several muscle and ligament groups are in use, particularly in counter-balancing the pulling forces of gravity. The muscles most used in standing still are those at the back of the neck that hold the head upright, lumbar spinal muscles that sustain the trunk of the body, and leg muscles that maintain the position of the feet at the ankle joints.

Because there is no obvious use of muscles or tendons in standing still, it may be quite difficult at first for the new meditator to be totally aware of the body in that position. Making a mental probe or 'sweep' of the body helps.

While in the standing position, before the commencement of walking meditation, the practitioner should take a couple of deep breaths and then let the breathing settle into its own regular pace. Awareness is then slowly swept over the entire length of the body, from head to feet and then back again, whilst acknowledging *standing... standing*. As meditation progresses and concentration increases, you will probably need to make this sweep only a couple of times. As a beginner you should make it as many times as necessary, and as slowly as necessary, until you are totally aware of the body in the standing position. Never allow the mental sweeps of the body to become simply a pre-meditation ritual: the sweeps *are* meditation.

During these sweeps, mentally probe the regions of the body which are most active in the standing position: the neck, the shoulders, the lower back, the thighs, the calves and ankles, and try to be be aware of the weight of the body on the feet. Finally, be aware of the body as a whole in the standing position – to actually know 'standing'. Move the awareness to the feet before commencing the first walking movement, as described in each exercise.

When in the standing position (and throughout walking meditation) the eyes should be open, downcast, and fixed on a point about two metres ahead. Although the eyes are open, they should not be focused on the floor surface. In some conditions the surface may be distracting – a patterned carpet or lino, for example – so the eyes should see only enough to let the brain know that the path is unobstructed.

There is often a temptation for beginners to look at their feet whilst in the standing position, and during walking meditation. This does not help and may cause a loss of concentration. Keep the unfocused gaze ahead of the feet.

When in the standing position, and during walking  meditation, the arms should be relaxed and unbent, with the hands loosely clasped in front of, or behind, the body. In front or behind doesn't matter – the point is that clasped hands will prevent the arms from swinging about, which is an unnecessary and distracting physical action.

Some meditation centres suggest that the hands may be clasped across the stomach, or that the arms may be folded across the chest. You may find these positions comfortable, but to bend the arms at the elbows to raise the hands higher will bring other muscle groups into use, which may be more tiring. However, try each arm and hand position to find the one that seems most conducive to your own practice.

Standing

In the standing position, the feet should be level and about three inches apart. Walking meditation (and sitting) should be undertaken shoeless and preferably bare-footed.

Turning movements

At the completion of each length of the walking path it is necessary to turn around so that the body is facing back down the path. Turning is usually made in three slow stages, traditionally clockwise. Some centres teach students to turn in more than three stages – it doesn't matter providing full mindfulness is kept on each movement.

Starting with the feet about three inches apart, an *intending to turn* acknowledgement is made as many times as necessary to really <u>know</u> the intention. There must be no movement while the 'intending to' acknowledgement is being made. If there is total awareness, the whole body may be felt to tense as the acknowledgement is made.

The right foot is then moved clockwise, one third of a semi-circle. There should be as little movement of the right heel as possible, and it should remain almost on the same spot throughout the turn. Practise keeping the right heel in the same position on the floor and just very slightly lifting and turning the rest of the foot. The foot needs to be lifted only sufficiently for it to brush across the floor surface. With this movement, *turning* is acknowledged once. The mental acknowledgement must be made while the foot is actually moving.

When the right foot has completed the first part of the turn, the left foot is then moved round parallel to the right, just brushing the floor, while at the same time another *turning* acknowledgement is made. The body is moved together with the left foot, but only very slight movement of the upper body is needed. After the first movement, the feet should still be about three inches apart. Make the pairs of movements three times, acknowledging *turning* with each movement. The turning movements should be followed by another few moments of standing still, whilst acknowledging *standing... standing... standing,* before recommencing the walking movements.

It is important to be thoroughly familiar with the turning procedure before starting walking meditation practice. The three pairs of movements in turning must bring you to the correct position facing back down the walking path, without the need for an extra half turn or distracting shuffling of the feet. It is also important that the feet should still be about three inches apart when the turn is complete. If the feet are so close together that the ankles touch, there will be an immediate distraction from the meditation, and a loss of concentration.

Sitting meditation

Positions

Some people make daily meditation a part of their lives and may continue to practise for many years. Some also regularly attend meditation classes or intensive residential retreats. Although in early practice the new meditator may sit for only short periods, perhaps as little as 15 or 20 minutes, as ability increases it is important to gradually extend the meditation time: 45 to 60 minutes is a reasonable length. But whether sitting in meditation for a short or long period, it is necessary that the chosen posture is not only comfortable and conducive to meditation, but also physiologically correct for the individual's body.

What may feel comfortable for a single period of sitting meditation may not be right in the long term and physical damage could eventually be caused, particularly to the knees and ankles. Proceed with care and take notice of any warning signs that the body gives. However, few Westerners are used to sitting cross-legged on the floor, so some minor aches and pains must be expected at first. These should disappear as the meditator becomes more experienced and the muscles and tendons adjust to unfamiliar use.

In meditation, small aches and pains may sometimes seem worse than they actually are. A few mental acknowledgements can often make them disappear, or at least diminish to the point where they can be ignored. Sharp pains, numbness and cramps should <u>not</u> be ignored. The position you have chosen to sit in may be exacerbating some physical problem of which you have previously been unaware. A change of position for future meditation should be considered.

All our bodies are different. Some are fat or thin, some people are 'round-shouldered', some are 'close-chested' and some have one leg shorter than the other. The meditator must find the position that most suits his or her own body, or adjust the body's deficiencies with cushions or pads. The new meditator should not immediately try to force the body into the 'full lotus' position; that may lead to intense discomfort, distraction and a consequent loss of concentration during meditation.

Meditation should never be an egotistic trial or test of how much pain can be endured. It is better to start off in a position in which you are sufficiently comfortable to be able to undertake the meditation, but not so comfortable that you fall asleep after a few minutes. You can then gradually work towards a better position over a period of months, perhaps in combination with physical exercises to loosen up the joints and muscles of the back, shoulders and legs.

Many meditators find it helpful to use a large, thin cushion for sitting meditation, but the cushion should be firm and supportive, rather than soft and squashy. The cushion should be large enough to give support not only to the buttocks, but to the knees and ankles as well.

The traditional and ideal position for sitting meditation is the 'full lotus': sitting cross-legged with each foot, sole uppermost, on the opposite thigh. Images of the Buddha often depict him in this way. The position gives the best balance to the body and is particularly suitable for long periods of sitting. However, anybody trying this for the first time is likely to need help getting 'undone' again, for although it is the ideal position it can be far from easy to get into and out of. It is better for the new meditator to use one of the other positions whilst trying to work towards the full lotus or half lotus. Don't feel that you must achieve the full lotus position – it is by no means essential and your meditation can progress just as well in the other positions. The main point is to be comfortable, balanced and mindful of whichever position is adopted.

The 'half lotus' is more easily achieved and maintained since it requires only one foot on the opposite thigh, whilst the other is folded flat on the floor.

If the half lotus is uncomfortable, one foot may rest on the opposite calf with the other foot folded on the floor.

Alternatively, both legs may simply be folded on the floor, tucked as far back into the body as possible.

To achieve the best balance in the full or half lotus positions, the knees should rest flat on the floor. Most beginners will find that theirs don't. Use an additional small, flat cushion placed under the buttocks to slightly raise and angle the body forward, but not enough that the upper part of the body is actually leaning forward. Smaller pads under the knees will give additional support, if required. Experiment as necessary with the placement of cushions and pads until the body is perfectly balanced; neither falling forwards nor backwards. You should be able to sit perfectly upright without any painful tensions or strains, especially in the neck and shoulders.

If sitting in any cross-legged position is difficult – for those suffering from rheumatism, for example – a straight-backed chair can be used. If using a chair, a book under each of its back legs is helpful to bring the body-weight forward slightly.

In all the positions, the spine should be as upright as far as its natural curvature allows. Don't try and make it ram-rod

Full lotus.   **Half lotus.**   **Both feet on floor.**

straight; it should be straight enough that the body neither slumps forward nor arches back. The head should be balanced on the spine, but can be inclined forward very slightly if there is a feeling of pressure on the back of the neck. The shoulders should be drawn back slightly, otherwise there is an inclination for the body to slump forward. If the body slumps the abdominal area will be compressed and the rise and fall of the abdomen will become less obvious.

The hands are usually placed in the lap, one resting on the other with the palms uppermost and the thumb-tips lightly touching. A small, flat pad placed in the lap for the hands to rest on can be helpful for some meditators. Sometimes, the hands may become too warm when resting on each other, in which case they can be placed flat on the knees.

Usually, in sitting meditation, the eyes are kept lightly closed and are directed slightly downwards. Some instructors suggest it is better that they remain open, or half open, with an unfocused gaze fixed on the floor about 2 metres ahead. Alternatively, the meditator may sit facing a blank wall with the eyes open – a method favoured by some Zen meditation schools. Try all the methods to see which is most helpful for your own practice.

The mouth should be relaxed with the lips held gently shut or very slightly open – whichever is most comfortable – but they should not be squeezed together and the teeth should not be clenched. The tongue should rest behind the lower teeth.

Before starting your meditation practice, try the various positions and experiment with cushions and pads. Sit for about 15 minutes, without meditating, but whilst mentally probing the body for potential discomfort points, especially in the neck, shoulders, back and knees.

The sitting down procedure

When you have decided on the sitting position you will meditate in, you should next practise the movements involved in changing from the standing position to the chosen sitting position.

The last movement of walking meditation is followed by a few moments of standing still (with acknowledgements) before slowly lowering the body into the sitting meditation position. Walking meditation should flow naturally into sitting meditation, with no break in awareness and no loss of concentration. The movements involved in the change of position are part of the meditation.

Practise going from the standing position to sitting, if possible at first watching the movements you make in a mirror. Practise several times, keeping to the same general procedure and mentally noting at which point you bend the knees, or stretch out a hand for support. You should be able to break your movements down into at least six very specific and acknowledged movements. The movements should be slow, but not awkwardly so. Aim at a speed where the movements are fluid, but still allow time for acknowledgements.

Lying meditation

There are two recommended positions for lying meditation – lying on the right side or lying flat on the back. The Buddha is said to have lain down on his right side when he knew he was close to death and continued to meditate in the position until he passed away. Images of the Buddha often depict him in the position, though are sometimes incorrectly described as the 'sleeping Buddha'.

Although lying meditation can be very beneficial, it can also quickly lead to sleep. In fact, many meditators who practise in the lying position do so at the end of the day as an aid to deep, relaxed sleep. If practised at the end of the day, lying meditation should not play a great part in a beginner's meditation programme. There seems little point in planning to meditate for 45 or 60 minutes if sleep follows after 15 minutes.

Lying meditation is better considered as an 'extra' to the normal sitting practice and as an aid to sleep, in which case it should be started 15-30 minutes before the meditator's normal sleeping time.

When lying on the right side, the right leg should be straight with the left leg, also straight, resting on it. The left arm should be placed along the body in line with the legs. The head should be supported by the bent right arm and open hand. Some meditators may prefer to lie on their left side, in which case the position of the arms and legs should be reversed. When lying on the left side, the heart-beat may be quite noticeable and can be a distraction for some people. The eyes should be lightly closed or half-open, without specific focus.

When lying on the back, the legs should be straight with the feet close together, but not touching. The arms should be straight at the sides and the palms flat to the bed surface.

As with sitting meditation, lying meditation is best undertaken after a period of walking meditation – perhaps 10 or 15 minutes. Just as the last step of walking before sitting meditation should bring you to the sitting cushion, so the last step before lying meditation should bring you to the lying place. The last step of walking should be followed by a few moments of standing still (with acknowledgements) and then the lying position should be taken up, using acknowledged movements, as when changing from standing to sitting.

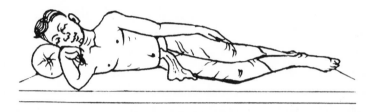

Lying position

If planning to meditate in the lying position before sleeping, the meditator may want to undress before getting into or onto the bed. The movements involved in undressing can be used as an extension of, or instead of, the walking practice to help maintain concentration, and should be undertaken in a similar way to the 'mindfulness exercises' described later in this chapter.

Lying meditation follows the same procedure as sitting practice. Objectively observe and acknowledge the rising and falling of the abdomen, or the in and out breaths at the nose, as well as all external stimuli and internal mental formations that arise. If a feeling of drowsiness arises, do not try to fight the feeling, nor give in to it. Just acknowledge *sleepy* and return the awareness to the rise and fall of the abdomen.

As your meditation progresses, lying practice can become very useful for starting off a new day mindfully. Unless you are someone who always gets up late and has to jump straight out of bed, a few minutes in the morning spent in meditation in the lying position can improve your outlook on the whole day.

Mindfulness exercises

Mindfulness exercises are an excellent method of improving concentration ability. For the new meditator especially, who may not have a high degree of developed mindfulness, the exercises can rapidly build up an awareness of many dozens of different bodily movements and intentions. Very ordinary activities can take on new meaning, at the same time as concentration is increased. Mindfulness exercises should be considered an integral part of your meditation programme, in conjunction with your usual walking, sitting and lying practice.

There is no particular importance attached to the activities themselves. The exercises are based on very mundane activities or chores which do not usually hold the interest, require little concentration, and which many people perform almost automatically.

For example, one exercise is taking a bath or shower. If you are in your own bathroom and familiar with the layout – where the light switch is, where the toothpaste is kept, etc – you do not have to give much thought to 'bath-time'. In the mindfulness exercise you do. Using mental acknowledgements for all intentions and actions, concentrate totally on every movement from the moment the bathroom door is opened. Acknowledge *intending to open… intending to open… opening…*

opening. Then *locking*. When turning on the taps, *twisting...* *twisting...* When testing the temperature of the water: *feeling...* *feeling*. When stepping into the bath: *lifting... lowering...* etc. This particular exercise is detailed further in chapter 8.

Suggested mindfulness exercises and a generalised procedure for each are given in the exercise chapters, but the principal of mindfulness can be used for any activity. Although the optimum time for a mindfulness exercise in this manual is about 30 minutes, a single activity need not be stretched to that length of time. Several shorter activities could be chosen instead. Even something that usually only takes moments, such as switching on a TV, can be an exercise in mindfulness, and the briefest of activities can be broken down into many intentions and movements.

6

Your meditative environment

The environment for all meditators, whether beginners or advanced, is of great importance, though may become less so as the practitioner gains in experience, and concentration and mindfulness increase.

Theoretically, an experienced meditator should be able to meditate anywhere and at any time, even in the busiest situations and noisiest environments. This is usually not so for the beginner. The new meditator rarely has sufficient mindfulness or developed concentration to cope with a lot of external stimuli, as well as all the internal mental phenomena that arise during meditation. For the new meditator, the right environment as free as possible of potential distractions can help to produce the calm and relaxed body and mind which is necessary for the most productive practice. Anything that helps the individual in his or her early practice should be considered. However, the 'right' environment needs careful thought, otherwise what appears at first to be a good place for meditation may actually hide subtle hindrances to long-term progress.

Most regular meditators undertake their practice at home. That is usually very convenient, but 'home' is frequently the source of many potential distractions. The home is where loved ones may also live and where many memories are based. Plans made for the future often concern our homes and those who live there. Home may be where many little daily dramas occur, and the meditator may also be surrounded by various temptations to break off the practice if it seems too difficult, or boring, or if there is insufficient commitment on any particular occasion. A break for a cup of coffee, a favourite radio or TV programme, a telephone call, or small chores that need doing, can all be used as excuses by the undisciplined mind to get involved with something that seems more immediately interesting or important than meditation practice. The new meditator should be aware of these potential practical and emotional hindrances and try to overcome them as much as possible. For example, get the most important chores out of the way, and out of the mind, before starting meditation. Make any telephone calls that need to be made, and try to deal with anything that may play on the mind and disturb the meditation.

If planning to meditate at home, choose one particular place to be your regular meditation area. In a perfect situation, an empty spare room is ideal, but even if you only make one small corner of a room your regular meditation place, that is helpful.

An environment as empty as possible of visual distractions is better than a cluttered one. Even though you will be practising sitting meditation with closed eyes, a favourite ornament or photograph seen just before closing the eyes may lead to memories, day-dreaming, and a loss of concentration.

A meditator told me that when he first started to practise he always sat in a corner of his room, facing a wall. His wallpaper was of a complex and colourful pattern and was the last thing he saw before closing his eyes. He said that he sometimes carried the image of the wallpaper into his meditation and that it made his mind 'busy'. He overcame it by pinning a plain white towel onto the wall, and he would simply sit looking at the towel for a few minutes, before closing his eyes and settling into his meditation. A small point, perhaps, but for that particular meditator it was a help.

Noise can be a major distraction, especially during walking meditation, so a quiet place is helpful. If you can unplug the telephone, so much the better. Although your meditation place should be as quiet as possible, don't put earplugs in, or headphones over the ears, to cut out external noise. You may become too aware of the natural and unceasing internal ear sounds. During walking meditation, it is better to try to dispassionately ignore external sounds, and all other external stimuli, and to work with them during sitting meditation (as explained in chapter 5). Meditators who live in crowded or busy homes may find it beneficial to get up earlier than the rest of the household, or go to bed later, and use that time when the environment is quiet as their meditation period.

Some meditators find that a dimly lit room is better than a brightly lit one. Use candles for lighting if you want, but don't deliberately set out to create a 'spiritual' or 'religious' atmosphere. That is unnecessary outward form and may become a hindrance to your long-term practice.

Buddhist meditators often have a small image of the Buddha in their homes. They may bow three times in front of it, and light candles and incense prior to starting their practice. This is not done to create a spiritual or religious ambience, but is the traditional way that Buddhists pay respect to the 'Triple Gem': the Teacher (Buddha), what he taught (the Dhamma), and the community of monks (the Sangha) who have preserved that teaching. Besides revering the historical Buddha, the bows, offerings and incense are a way of fixing the mind on the *qualities* of Buddha-hood – the same qualities that we should all be endeavouring to cultivate through meditation.

Even if you do not consider yourself Buddhist in a religious sense, there is no reason why you should not adopt the practice of paying respect to the Triple Gem, since it is not an act of worship. If adopted, the process of paying respect should be done mindfully and as part of your meditation. You should be aware that you are offering traditional gifts of light and incense to the memory of the man who, through compassion, devoted much of his life to teaching what he discovered – including your meditation. Bows and offerings mindfully made can help concentrate the mind before starting meditation.

The temperature of the room in which you plan to meditate should not be too high, nor too low. Your body and mind will become lethargic if the room is too warm or stuffy, and you will be distracted by physical discomfort if too cold. In either case, you will be unable to maintain the energy and determination needed for practice. A room slightly cooler than usual, and with a source of fresh air, is ideal.

The clothes worn during meditation can make a difference for some people. Don't wear tight-fitting clothing which you may feel against the skin. Very loose clothing is better – something like a bathrobe or dressing gown could be ideal. If wearing trousers, loosen or remove the belt. All meditation should be undertaken without shoes, and preferably bare-footed.

Even when practising at home, some meditators like to wear white clothes for their meditation. Some meditation centres may insist on it during organised retreats. On meditation retreats, particularly at Buddhist monasteries, meditators usually live within the eight moral precepts, and the wearing of white is taken to be a sign of moral and spiritual purity. If you choose to wear white for your meditation at home, you should not allow yourself to believe that by doing so you have suddenly become morally and spiritually 'pure'. It is just outward form and is really of little or no meaning, even if the meditator has also taken the eight precepts. Only the <u>practice</u> can bring purity. (White clothing does have some practical value on a retreat since non-retreat visitors to the monastery or centre will know that those wearing white are not permitted to talk, except in necessity).

A lady meditator who had a secluded garden told me that in warm weather she liked to meditate there without clothes. She said she enjoyed the sensation of the air on her skin and the 'sense of freedom' it gave her. Sadly, the lady had missed the point of true mental development and was more concerned with sensuality. I know other meditators who practise privately without clothing, or just wearing a sarong, but if you are tempted to do so you should investigate your reasons carefully.

Sometimes during meditation, new practitioners may become very aware of the feeling of clothing against the skin. This may become a constant distraction for some. If that is so in your case, and if you believe your meditation will be better without the feeling of clothing against the skin, then try it – but don't do it because it 'feels good'. You will be setting up a major hindrance for yourself and the meditation may become an end in itself, rather than the means to an end. Also, if you extend your practice by attending meditation classes or residential retreats, you will not be able to strip off as you may by then have become accustomed to doing. Loose-fitting clothing is usually better than no clothing at all.

During sitting meditation especially, the practitioner may become very conscious of the feel and weight of spectacles, rings or other jewelry. It is better to remove them before starting practice, as well as emptying pockets of loose change, keys and other objects.

In sitting meditation, the hands are usually placed in the lap. In walking meditation they are often clasped in front of the body. If wearing a watch, it is therefore very easy and tempting to keep sneaking a look to see how much time has passed. It is better to remove your watch before starting practice. An alarm clock is necessary if planning to meditate for a specific length of time, but it should be somewhere in the room where the alarm can be heard, but the clock cannot be seen by opening the eyes or turning the head.

Timing of one's meditation can present a small practical problem when meditating at home. A pre-fixed period of walking meditation usually precedes a pre-fixed period of sitting, so two alarm clocks are needed; one to ring at the end of the walking period and the other at the end of the sitting period. However, having two alarm clocks is preferable to breaking concentration by looking at a clock during walking meditation, or opening the eyes to check the time during sitting, or re-setting a single clock between the two types of meditation.

Many apartments or houses do not have an ideal length of space for walking meditation. If possible, the walking path should be 12'- 15' long, without obstruction, and with an easily recognisable beginning and end, so that there is no need to count paces. Usually, walking meditation paths are straight and the meditator turns at each turn to return down the same path. If this is not possible in your own home environment, there is nothing wrong with a shorter length, or you can use an L-shaped path. In the latter case, you will need to make a half-turn at the angle, adapting the usual full-turn movements, but using similar mental acknowledgements. Whatever the shape of the path, it should have a point at each end where you can make the full turning movements easily.

Try to arrange your walking path so that you can take at least 10-12 short steps before needing to turn. The path should be free of obstructions, such as furniture, loose mats and loose cats. The eyes are kept open during walking meditation, so if you have a choice it is better to walk on a plain surface rather than patterned carpet or lino. 'Busy' patterns can more easily distract the eye and diminish concentration. There should be some neutral object, such as a book, on the floor at each end of the path which you will recognise as marking the turning point.

The final length of the walking path should ideally bring you to the sitting meditation place. This may be impractical for some people. Some meditators use a hall or garden path for walking meditation, but may undertake their sitting meditation in another place or room. If you are able to undertake both types of meditation in the same general area, that is helpful, but if not you should proceed from one place to the other as a continuation of walking meditation, acknowledging each step. If you need to open and close doors, do so mindfully (as you will do in the mindfulness exercises). If you need to go up or down stairs, pause in your walking meditation, acknowledge *standing* for a few moments, and then *lifting* as each foot is raised to go up stairs, or *lowering* as you go downstairs. The point is not to lose any of the concentration you have built up during walking meditation when moving from the main walking path to your sitting place.

Besides your walking and sitting meditation at home, it can be very beneficial to practise sitting or contemplative meditation in other environments. Meditation outdoors, in a park or in the countryside for example, can be very beneficial. However, because the environment may be so pleasant, rather than neutral, it is easy to be led into discursive thought and to lose mindfulness to pleasant external stimuli. The practitioner should be aware of that potential hindrance. Some outdoor environments can be more broadly useful to overall and long-term progress, and can help give the beginner a greater and more vivid understanding of what the practice is about.

For example, when I lived in a forest monastery in Thailand, I used to meditate near a disused irrigation ditch. This was a miles-long concrete channel about nine feet wide and about five feet deep. Not exactly a river, but the water was flowing and the channel contained many plants, rocks, fish and all the components of a river. Before my formal sitting meditation, I would spend about 15 minutes just watching the river flow by, and contemplating the continuous change that was taking place. The river was always the river, but it was never exactly the same river for two consecutive moments. In places, the water flowed smoothly, then it tumbled over rocks, or its current was disturbed by plants that moved lazily beneath the surface. Small fish darted about like random thoughts, never still for a moment. The river was impermanent and in constant flux.

After a short time watching the river, I would raise my eyes to a small chain of mountains a few kilometres away and I found it easy to apply that same perception to the mass of granite on the horizon. Although the mountains appeared permanent and unchanging, I could visualise the erosion that was continuously taking place. Sun, wind and rain attacked the rock, small animals burrowed into the earth, tree roots forced the granite apart, and so on. Although I could not see any change, I was aware that, like the river, even the mountains were not the same from one moment to the next. They were impermanent and subject to constant change and deterioration.

Through such observation, it became easier to apply that same perception of impermanence to my own physical body and mental processes. Physically, I could not perceive change in myself from moment to moment, yet it was continuing ceaselessly. And not just the physical body, for my mental activities also were never the same for two consecutive moments. Thoughts were constantly rising and ceasing, impermanent and in constant flux. There was as little permanent 'self' to be found within my body as there was in the river, or in the mountains. Even phenomena which have apparent permanence are inherently impermanent and conditioned; how much more so our own physical bodies, situations, emotions and mental processes. After my period of contemplation, I would settle into my meditation, watching the internal 'river' of my own mind as it constantly flowed by.

Few meditators are likely to live near a river with a handy chain of mountains, but similar contemplation as a prelude to your practice can be undertaken in any natural environment. You can even sit for a few minutes looking at a tree or a single flower, and try to really understand how it is born, grows old, withers, dies and returns to the earth. Applying that same perception to your own body and your mental activities can make your meditation more pointed, more dynamic.

Cemeteries, especially old ones, also make excellent meditative or contemplative environments. Again, the meditator should be aware of the dangers of discursive thinking in the environment and must keep an objective mind about what is seen. There is nothing gloomy or pessimistic about such contemplation – in fact, it is very much part of the Buddha's teaching. The meditator is merely dispassionately observing the nature of the physical body, and hence all conditioned phenomena. Spend a few minutes walking round the cemetery and reading the headstones; the 'born' and 'died' dates. Some people lived a long time, some a short time, some hardly at all, but all were born, grew older, died and lie rotting in the ground. In some very old cemeteries, the carved granite headstones may be so ancient that the words themselves may have been worn away by wind and rain and can no longer be read, or the headstones may be cracked, broken and fallen. Graves which were once well tended may have become neglected, unvisited and forgotten by those who once loved and mourned the deceased. Physical conditions and mental phenomena, all constantly changing, conditioned and impermanent. That perception can be applied to your own physical body, and to the arising and passing away of your own emotions and other mental phenomena; impermanent and subject to constant change.

7

Your meditation programme

Progress in meditation is an individual matter. It is not necessarily true that the more you do it, the quicker you will progress. Your progress will have less to do with the number of hours spent practising, and more with your personal commitment and energy, as well as the attitude you start out with. These are decisive factors. For the beginner, meditation can seem to be both extremely difficult and very, very boring. In fact, it seems difficult only because your conditioned mind *tells* you it is boring; because you have conditioned concepts about what constitutes 'boring' and 'interesting'. There is nothing particularly difficult about sitting still for 15 minutes, 45 minutes, or even an hour, just being aware of the abdomen rising and falling, but most people are used to filling their time with what they consider to be more interesting activities.

When you have to force yourself to meditate; when the thought, "I could be down the pub, or watching TV" is uppermost in your mind, then you are fighting an internal battle with yourself and can make little or no progress. Ten minutes – even five minutes – of sitting with a clear, aware mind, is better than an hour sitting with clenched teeth waiting for the alarm clock to ring.

So, although perseverance and diligence are important, it must be with the right attitude – which is *no attitude* at all. Put in neither too little effort, nor too much. When sitting, just sit. That's all there is to it, really. Just to sit and dispassionately observe. Do not aim for particular 'results'. Both expectation of, and striving for, particular goals can be a hindrance. If the desired goal is not achieved, the meditator may develop a sense of failure, impatience or disappointment – all hindrances to progress. Demand nothing, have no expectations, no sense of anticipation, nor feelings of disappointment. Both the desire or clinging to succeed, and aversion to failure, are obstacles to progress in meditation.

Although meditation is a progressive development of the mind, each 'sitting' is a meditation period in its own right. Comparisons between today's meditation and yesterday's are mostly meaningless. Thinking that today you are 'better' at meditation than yesterday, or that yesterday's sitting was more successful than today's, or maybe that tomorrow's will be even better, will take you nowhere. Today's meditation is as it is; yesterday's was as it was, and tomorrow's – who knows? In each sitting, the meditator must be aware only of how things are in the present moment. Judgmental and comparative thinking are unnecessary and will become an obstacle to progress. However, for the absolute beginner practising without an instructor or guide, a periodic and <u>objective</u> review of overall progress is helpful, especially when considering moving on to a more demanding meditation exercise.

As your interest in meditation develops, you may meet others who also meditate. Meditators should be cautious about discussing their progress, or lack of it, in any great detail with other meditators. There is nothing secret in meditation, but care must be taken to avoid comparisons between one's own progress and another's. Meditators progress at different rates, so comparisons are usually worthless and can lead to competitive and egotistic feelings, or feelings of personal success or failure. However, if you have an experienced instructor or guide, you should honestly and openly discuss all aspects of your meditation with him or her.

How long should you meditate?

To gain even the most superficial benefits from meditation, regular daily practice is essential. How much time you devote to practice depends, of course, on how much time you can spare in your daily routine. Although you may start off with much shorter meditation periods, you should certainly be aiming for at least 30 minutes each for walking and sitting each day, plus a total of about 30 minutes for a mindfulness exercise, then a short period of lying meditation immediately before sleeping.

'Time' whilst in meditation can seem to pass very quickly, but for the beginner it may seem to drag interminably. You must learn patience, and while you are in meditation it should be of no concern to you how much time has passed. Your alarm clock will ring to warn you of the end of your practice, and you should put such thoughts out of your mind and continue to sit to the end of the pre-set time (and longer, if you are able). It is very important that the new practitioner should start to discipline the mind from the very first practice. Not giving in to apparent boredom is the first lesson to be learned – and the hardest.

Initially, an hour or more of meditation each day may be too much for some new practitioners to cope with, but it is not necessary to plunge straight into long periods. Build up slowly, perhaps starting off with only 15 minutes of walking followed by 15 minutes of sitting, with a short mindfulness exercise during the day and a few minutes of lying meditation at the end of the day. In that case, the total of 30 minutes spent in walking and sitting should be a continuous period. It will not be so beneficial to allocate 15 minutes in the morning for walking meditation, and then 15 minutes in the evening for sitting. Walking meditation should always immediately precede sitting, since the concentration built up during walking is used in the sitting practice. The mindfulness exercises can be considered as an 'extra' to your normal meditation programme and can be undertaken at any time.

It can be worthwhile to write yourself a meditation programme covering several months in advance, in which you gradually plan to extend your meditation times. A written programme can also help reinforce a sense of commitment in the new meditator. If you decide to make such a programme, it must be considered only as a guide, and not something you must rigidly adhere to. As you practise, adapt the programme as necessary, depending on the development of your mindfulness and concentration ability. For example, for the first two weeks, plan to meditate each day for perhaps 15 minutes each in walking and sitting. For the third and fourth weeks, plan to extend that time to 20 minutes for each, in the fifth and sixth weeks to 25 minutes, etc. But when using such a programme, remember that your meditation is not a trial or test of how long you can sit in one position, or walk slowly. If you find your concentration has not developed sufficiently to enable you to cope with longer meditation periods, then reduce your time a little until your concentration ability has improved. Remember that the <u>quality</u> of your meditation is more important than the amount of time spent doing it. Whatever the length of time you plan to meditate for, don't give up at the very first feeling of boredom, or at the first minor ache you feel. You must persevere and 'stretch yourself' – but not force yourself – if you are to make progress.

Generally, the beginner's walking and sitting meditation should be of the same duration. As the practitioner gains experience and mindfulness increases, a different balance may be more beneficial. Sometimes an instructor, who knows the practitioner's progress, will advise extending the walking meditation time and reducing the sitting time, or vice versa. Too much concentration built up during walking meditation may sometimes adversely affect the sitting practice, but insufficient concentration may also cause sitting to be less productive. Because progress is such an individual matter, it is impossible to generalise about the balance any particular meditator should try to achieve. However, this is not something that usually affects the beginner in early practice and you should balance your walking and sitting times equally.

As a beginner, your walking and sitting meditation should ideally be undertaken at approximately the same time each day. It makes no difference what time of day, but choose a convenient time and try to keep to it. Never let your meditation become routine, or a chore; something you have to squeeze in between 'more important' activities, nor a habit or ritual like a morning coffee break.

Many people feel lethargic after having eaten a meal, so immediately after eating is not the best time to meditate. If you meditate in the evening, allow a couple of hours after dinner or supper before starting your practice.

If you find you have the odd ten minutes or so to spare during the day, spending that time in sitting meditation will relax the body and mind and can help towards more beneficial meditation at your usual and longer practice time. Such short periods will not upset the balance of your meditation. Some people use the time in going to work on a bus or train as an additional meditation time. There is no need to sit on your seat in the full lotus position; just sit upright with the eyes closed and the hands in the lap, watching the rise and fall of the abdomen.

Meditation classes and retreats

Most people lead busy lives and are unable to set aside more than an hour or so each day for meditation. For the beginner, being mindful usually means doing things unnaturally slowly, breaking down every action in order to be fully aware and to mentally acknowledge the individual movements. This is usually not very practical for extended periods during the daily routine, and the enthusiastic beginner should try to set aside an evening or two each week to attend regular meditation classes with an experienced instructor or guide.

The best starting point to find a suitable centre will be the Buddhist Society of your particular country. These societies are usually able to offer advice about the various major centres and their activities, and some publish handbooks which may have very comprehensive listings, city by city, and which are updated every year.

The annual handbook of the Buddhist Society of Great Britain wisely commences with a warning that inclusion of any particular teacher, group or centre does not imply endorsement by the Society. This is an important point, whichever country you live in. If you are in search of an experienced and wise meditation instructor, you should not necessarily go to a particular centre just because it happens to be conveniently located. There are many well-meaning instructors with some knowledge, but little wisdom, teaching 'meditation'. Although the practitioner will not come to any harm by studying with such an instructor, in the long term it may be counter-productive. Your meditation is important and a good instructor or centre is worth travelling to.

To get the maximum benefit from meditation, the serious practitioner will also consider attending first a few one- or two-day retreats, and then a longer and more intensive retreat. Retreats usually provide the ideal environment for meditation. They allow practitioners to cut themselves off entirely from many outside stimuli, and to practise intensively under the guidance of an experienced instructor. A retreat may be for as little as a day, but often they are residential and last a week, or longer. Depending on the centre, residential retreats may be very intensive indeed, and are usually geared more towards experienced meditators than beginners. Some centres will not allow new meditators to undertake a residential retreat until they have attended at least several one- or two-day retreats first. It is wise to discuss the retreat with the organisers before making a commitment to attend.

Some of the most well organised one-day retreats, and longer residential retreats, are held at Buddhist monasteries, often with Buddhist monks as instructors. These monks have frequently been trained by recognised Meditation Masters, often in the Thai or Burmese traditions, and have a high level of commitment in their teaching. Although held in Buddhist monasteries, the retreats usually have little religious content and meditators of other faiths should not feel any sense of compromising their own beliefs by attending such centres. Retreats at Buddhist monasteries are available to, and suitable for, people of all religious faiths. The daily routine on a residential retreat may include a short period when respect is paid to the memory of the Buddha and his Teaching, but this is not an act of worship and no attempt is ever made at

Buddhist monasteries to convert meditators to Buddhism. All faiths are respected by Buddhists.

Attending a residential retreat, or even a single day retreat, requires a strong sense of commitment. The routine is often based on monastic discipline, even when the retreat is not held in a monastery. Rising is usually very early, talking and socialising with other meditators may be discouraged, reading and writing may not be allowed and sometimes only vegetarian food is served, often with the last meal before noon. But this discipline does help to create the right mental conditions needed for intensive practice.

Those who attend retreats may be expected to wear white clothes, though this is not always compulsory and at some centres the clothes may be provided. Those who come are usually expected to spend the period of the retreat living under 8 traditional rules (the Eight Precepts) which are considered the moral basis for meditation practice. The Precepts are:

1. To abstain from killing any living being.
2. To abstain from stealing.
3. To abstain from all sexual activity.
4. To abstain from false speech.
5. To abstain from intoxicants and drugs.
6. To abstain from eating solid food after midday.
7. To abstain from seeking entertainment, and the wearing of perfumes, jewellery and personal adornment.
8. To abstain from using luxurious beds and high seats. (In modern terms, to abstain from unnecessary luxuries and comforts).

There may be other rules that individual centres request those who attend retreats to follow. Those who intend to come should enquire about such rules before making a commitment to attend.

Meditation instruction at Buddhist monasteries is usually free, although a charge may be made for food on residential retreats. Some private meditation centres are run on more commercial lines and may make additional charges as well.

When seeking a weekly meditation class, retreat centre, or discussion and meeting group, it should be remembered that there are two schools of Buddhism: Theravada and Mahayana, the latter including the many and varied Zen schools. The Theravada and Mahayana schools teach with the same primary goals and exist in harmony together, though there are differences of emphasis in some aspects of the teaching and in meditation techniques. Before deciding on a centre to attend, or group to join, it would be wise for the new meditation practitioner, or new Buddhist, to undertake some research into the two schools.

8

The practice

It is important that the meditation exercises in this section are practised in the order they are presented. Don't be tempted to jump ahead because you believe you are capable of the more complex exercises. Check your ego! Your concentration and mindfulness should be developed slowly, systematically and carefully if you are to make genuine progress.

There are seven exercises in this section, but it should not be considered that this represents a course covering seven weeks, seven months, or even seven years. Any new meditator who treats it that way, and sets out to achieve 'results' within a certain period is likely to create an obstacle to progress before even starting the practice.

The exercises have suggested duration times, but these are *optimum* times and something for the beginner to work towards over a number of weeks, or months. As suggested in the previous chapter, write yourself a meditation programme covering two months or so in advance, in which your meditation time is gradually increased. If you start off with a meditation time of 15 minutes each for walking and sitting, and increase that time by 5 minutes each week, you will be working with Exercise 1 for four weeks – but even then you should not automatically move on to Exercise 2.

Before deciding whether to move from one exercise to the next, review your practice as objectively as you can. Over the weeks or months of practising your current exercise, have you gradually become aware of less occasions of daydreaming and mind-wandering? Do distractions lead to lengthy discursive thinking, or are you able to acknowledge and let go of the distractions increasingly easily and completely? Have you been able to extend your periods of one-pointedness, of staying with the walking movements or rise and fall of the abdomen? In the mindfulness exercises, are you acknowledging gradually more intentions and actions? Do you give up quickly at the first feeling of boredom or physical discomfort, or are you increasingly able to persevere?

If you genuinely feel you are ready to move on, and are capable of a more complex exercise, then do so. But there's no point fooling yourself (or letting your ego fool you). If you think your mindfulness has not improved sufficiently, then stay with your present exercise. This is particularly important after Exercise 2, when the sitting and lying practice become increasingly complex. The later walking exercises can be practised with the earlier sitting and lying exercises to increase concentration. Some meditators find it unnecessary ever to proceed beyond Exercise 2 in sitting and lying meditation, since the benefits of even the more simple exercises may soon become apparent if they are practised with a sufficiently high level of mindfulness.

Whilst practising without an instructor or guide, the new meditator should make such an objective and honest review before moving on to any new exercise. There is no need to feel any sense of failure or disappointment if your concentration level and ability do not seem to have improved. If that is the case, however, you should also examine other aspects of your meditation programme as well.

Is your meditation environment as quiet as it could be, and as free of distractions as possible? Are you meditating at a good time of day, a time when your mind is relaxed? Or are you squeezing in your meditation between other responsibilities or chores you feel you should be getting on with? Is you sitting position uncomfortable, causing distracting fidgeting or frequent changes of position? Is it *too* comfortable, causing your body and mind to become lethargic? Is your meditation becoming too much like a habit, or simply a relaxation exercise?

There could be some less obvious reason for your lack of progress. Is there some long-term business, family business, or personal problem that is constantly at the back of your mind, causing you to practise your meditation with a background of restlessness and worry? Are you subconsciously harbouring some deep-rooted resentment, ill will or anger against some person, thing or situation which is constantly playing on your mind? Do you have sceptical doubts about the benefits of meditation practice, or some aspect of the Buddha's teaching? These are all hindrances to your meditation and must be cleared away before genuine progress can be made.

Persevere, and your concentration and mindfulness will improve.

As the meditator gains experience and concentration ability increases, mental sensations may sometimes arise that can be strange and quite intense. This is normal in meditation. Sometimes, a feeling of great joy may arise and the meditator may want to attach to it, to hold on to it in the mind. Do not. Observe impartially, acknowledge the feeling as *joy*, and return awareness to the rise and fall of the abdomen. Similarly, very intense feelings of sadness may arise. Do not struggle to force them out. Observe as dispassionately as possible, acknowledge *sadness,* and return awareness to the rise and fall of the abdomen.

Other sensations may, or may not arise. There may seem to be flashes of light, or visions of great beauty or ugliness. Do not be concerned about these mental phenomena (known as **nimitr** or **nimitta**). The beginner is not likely to experience them but, if they do arise, follow the same procedure: observe dispassionately, acknowledge them, and return to the rise and fall of the abdomen. Do not allow yourself to be frightened of the nimitr, but do not indulge in them. There may sometimes be odd physical sensations too: feelings of itchiness on the skin, or ·a burning sensation. Again, dispassionately observe, acknowledge the sensation, and return to the rise and fall of the abdomen. If you do experience strong sensations or visions, you should seek the advice of an experienced meditation instructor. These nimitr or sensations that arise generally follow a natural progression and are well known to most instructors. There is nothing sinister or dangerous about them, and nothing 'spiritual'. They are simply indications of new levels of concentration, but they may lead the meditator's practice into a dead end. Without a guide or instructor you may not be able to make further progress.

When some meditators have overcome the initial and very difficult period of their practice, and as they start to more fully understand what they are doing, they may begin to experience a sense of depression, unhappiness or frustration outside of their meditation.

As meditation progresses and wisdom begins to develop, the true nature of your mind will start to reveal itself to you. You may begin to recognise just how much craving, clinging, aversion and delusion your mind contains. Recognising it may be easier than overcoming it. That is the point when many meditators give up, rather than 'face up'. But the meditator should persevere. It is necessary to see and recognise the defilements and hindrances of the mind before they can be eradicated.

It's perhaps rather like a man who trips over something and falls heavily to the ground. He may be instinctively and intellectually aware that he has almost certainly damaged himself in some way, even though he is not yet aware of much pain. Then he rolls up his trouser leg and sees the extent of the injury – perhaps a gash, bruise, or swelling – and he is immediately (and frequently only then) aware of the associated pain. But he has to see the wound, examine it and clean it before it can heal.

Similarly, the meditator must observe his or her mental hindrances, examine them objectively, and cleanse the mind of them, before the mind can heal and function properly. As the meditator continues to persevere in his or her practice, and as Insight-Wisdom arises, so also will the hindrances be eradicated.

Letting go

'Letting go' is a much used term in meditation. Instructors and manuals, including this one, talk of acknowledging and then letting go of the various physical and mental phenomena that arise during Vipassana meditation. This letting go could sum up the whole purpose of meditation practice. When we learn to genuinely and completely let go, when we totally eradicate our egotistic delusions and cease our clinging, craving and aversion, and hence the unwholesome responses that arise from them, we truly experience Nibbana: total freedom of mind.

It is relatively easy in meditation to let go of physical sensations, discursive thinking and daydreaming, but some emotions that arise can be considerably more difficult. For the beginner, very strong or intense emotions do not usually arise unless they have been preceded by a lot of unacknowledged discursive thinking, and have gradually built from less extreme beginnings.

If during meditation you find yourself experiencing an intense emotion, you simply have to acknowledge and then make the effort to drag yourself away and return to the rise and fall of the abdomen. This may be impossible if the emotion is overwhelmingly strong. Then the only thing to do is to stop the meditation, since otherwise you will be constantly pulled back to the emotion which may continue to grow in intensity.

As soon as you stop meditating, you should objectively contemplate the emotion in an effort to analyse why it arose, and the thoughts that led to it. Although examining it in this intellectual way will not necessarily make it disappear, the meditator may see that it had no real or logical foundation. On the other hand, the meditator may be able to identify some emotional problem that he or she had previously been unaware of, or which had been pushed to the 'back of the mind'. Strong emotions will not usually arise if the meditator makes the right effort to develop mindfulness sufficiently to 'let go' in the earlier stages of the arising.

The development of this 'letting go' skill is very important, as the skill is carried over into daily life and the situations we all encounter from time to time.

We may find ourselves in a situation where we feel, for example, intense anger, ill-will, envy, or some other emotion that can cause conditioned, unwise and unwholesome response. To be able to control such emotions in their earlier and less extreme stages obviously makes the overcoming or letting go of them that much easier. It is easier, for example, to let go of a feeling of slight irritation than one of extreme anger. It is easier to let go of a feeling of slight sadness than one of overwhelming grief.

However, sometimes when we think we have let some particular emotion or mental response go, all the mind has done is overlaid and suppressed the emotion with some more 'positive' or wholesome one. Anger, for example, may be suppressed under happy thoughts and the outward projection of a smile and cheerful voice. That isn't letting go – it's 'covering up'. Beneath the outward appearance of calm, the anger may still be simmering away, continuing to cause mental suffering and sure to return at some future time.

But as your skill at letting go of less extreme thoughts, emotions and conditioning develops, you may one day quite unexpectedly find yourself taking a mental step back from some situation or phenomenon, and genuinely and completely letting go. You will have acted with developed wisdom and it can be an extraordinary feeling, just as though a heavy, crushing burden was quite suddenly removed from the shoulders.

The same thing can happen with other deep-rooted hindrances: resentment, ill-will, bitterness and envy. Sometimes such resentments have been harboured in the mind for a long time; sometimes so far back in the mind that we hardly know they are there any more, or have forgotten the original reason for their arising and development. Even though we may not always be consciously aware of them, they may nevertheless constantly affect our physical and verbal actions and responses.

When the mind genuinely lets go, the emotion can be seen and felt to be instantly evaporating, leaving behind a stillness which the mind may never have experienced before. It is not an empty stillness, for the mind is filled with profound peace, and a happiness that goes far beyond the normal mundane meaning of that word.

It doesn't follow that after the first time, you can repeat the experience whenever necessary, far less hold on to it, grasp it, as a permanent state. The more the meditator strives, or craves to let go, the more the object is defeated. But letting go does happen, and it may happen progressively more often. It isn't something you can learn to do. It can only develop through your meditation and the continual observance, recognition and letting go of lesser emotions. Ask any experienced meditator how to let go, and he or she is likely to respond: "You just let go". Which is the only answer.

Metta contemplation

In addition to your walking and sitting meditation, you should spend a few minutes at the end of your sitting practice contemplating 'metta'. Metta is usually translated from the Pali as 'loving kindness', or 'universal good will', and is one of the Four States of Consciousness which meditators should try to cultivate.

Metta is the desire that oneself, and all other beings, should be free from enmity, ill-will and suffering, and should be happy. Most of us like or love others to whom we are attached through the family, or who have qualities that we, as individuals, find attractive or admire. For many different reasons, we are happy to be with such people, enjoy our relationships with them, and become attached to them. We may also be very forgiving when the relationships don't run smoothly, and very understanding when our friends or loved ones exhibit less-than-admirable qualities. All of us find some people very easy to like, or love.

On the other hand, there are people, or types of people, whom we personally do not find attractive or admirable, and who do not have what we personally think of as virtuous qualities.

Generally, we do not like such people, don't want to know them or spend time with them, and are less forgiving of their human foibles. We may even feel great aversion to them. But even the people we do not like, or find unattractive for various reasons, suffer dukkha in all the same ways that we do, and for all the same reasons. They want the same basic things that all of us want: happiness, love, good health, freedom and so on.

The cultivation of metta, or universal good will, does not mean that we must force ourselves to like or love everybody in the world, even those in whom we can see no likeable qualities. That would simply be replacing one set of conditioning with another. There is little genuine value to ourselves or others if all we are doing is covering up our real feelings under a thin veneer. Instead, we should try to see the roots of our aversions, overcome them through meditation, and see those we are inclined to dislike in at least a more neutral way, without enmity or ill-will, and with understanding of their suffering.

During the evening service at Buddhist monasteries, monks usually chant a Pali verse concerning metta, and whilst chanting should be contemplating its meaning. This practice is often followed at meditation and retreat centres by group chanting after the meditation. Unfortunately, for some people, this chanting degenerates into a mere post-meditation ritual, and is of little value (especially as most meditators do not understand the Pali words they are chanting). For the new meditator, especially when practising alone and at home, it is better to simply sit quietly for a few moments at the end of the Vipassana practice, and to really try to contemplate metta; to really try to have understanding of others' suffering.

When your sitting practice has ended, move the hands to the knees as instructed in the exercises, and sit with the eyes closed. Try to call up the feeling of love by mentally imaging the person or people who you most love – perhaps husband or wife, parents, or children. Feel the warmth of that love within you; let it suffuse you, but then try to concentrate on the feeling itself without attaching to the individuals for whom you feel it most.

Try to extend that feeling to the types of people that you find likeable or admirable, and then to the types for whom your feelings are more neutral. Finally, to the types that you would not normally like, or admire, or feel aversion to. Try to hold that feeling of love, whilst thinking compassionately of all the people of the world, regardless of nationality, colour or religion, regardless of whether they are clever or stupid, attractive or unattractive, young or old, regardless of whether they like or dislike you, regardless of <u>anything</u>.

"Sabbe satta avera hontu"
"May all beings be free of enmity."
"Sabbe satta abyapajja hontu"
"May all beings be free from ill-will."
"Sabbe satta anugha hontu"
"May all beings be free from suffering."
"Sabbe satta sukhi attanan pariharantu"
"May all beings keep their own happiness."

Exercise 1

Walking meditation (1ˢᵗ stage)

Optimum duration: 30 minutes (or your own shorter, pre-set time).
Acknowledgement words: *standing... right goes thus... left goes thus... turning.* Plus acknowledgements of sitting down movements before commencing sitting meditation.

In Exercise 1 you will be concentrating mindfulness on each foot as it is moved forward. You are not concerned in this exercise with acknowledging any other walking movement, nor with intentions to move.

In the simplest analysis, you might assume that taking a step forward consists of three movements: lifting the foot, moving it forward, and lowering it. That is not the case, as will be seen in later exercises. However, because you might be aware of these three movements, there is the temptation to acknowledge *right* as the foot is lifted, *goes* as it is moved forward, and *thus* as it is lowered. That is not the correct procedure. The complete acknowledgement *right goes thus* (or *left goes thus*) <u>must</u> be made only whilst the foot is in motion forward. There is no acknowledgement in this exercise of either the lifting or lowering movements.

When walking normally, the movements of the feet are very fluid, each foot following the other without pause. Usually, as the leading foot is treading flat to the floor, so the heel of the following foot is already rising from the floor surface. In first stage walking meditation, it is important that each foot should have completed all its movements before there is any movement in the other foot. The heel, in particular, must not make any movement until the preceding foot is flat to the floor. Preventing the heel from automatically rising before the other foot has finished its movement necessitates a much shorter step than usual, and walking considerably more slowly than you would normally.

In Exercise 1, follow this procedure:

1. Take up the standing position at the beginning of your walking path, facing down the path. The eyes are open, and fixed without specific focus on the floor about 2 metres ahead. Allow your awareness to sweep over the body from head to feet, and then from feet to head, mentally probing those parts most in use in the standing position. Don't just think about it, actually try to place the whole of your awareness in the different parts of the body. Move the awareness back to the feet, being aware of the whole body in the standing position, whilst acknowledging *standing... standing... standing.*

2. Raise the right foot a few inches, but do not raise it straight up. Let the heel come up off the floor, as it would in normal walking, and raise the foot at a slight downward angle. The knee will bend slightly as the heel is first raised, then the toes leave the floor. Move the foot forward a shorter than normal pace. As the foot moves forward, acknowledge *right goes thus.* Lower the foot to the floor. The acknowledgement *right goes thus* must only be made whilst the foot is moving forward – not when it is being raised, or lowered. When the right foot is fully flat to the floor, only then should

the heel of the left foot be allowed to leave the floor surface. Raise the foot, move it forward whilst acknowledging *left goes thus*, and lower it to the floor. Continue this procedure to the end of the walking path.

3. After a few steps it is likely you will find your attention has already been distracted from the movements of the feet, either by some external sensory stimuli, or by thoughts arising in the mind. Try to ignore the distraction – do not acknowledge it – and immediately return your concentration to the movements of the feet. If the distraction is very great, stop walking, bring the feet together and acknowledge *standing… standing… standing.* It is not necessary to make the mental sweeps of the body, but be aware of the body in the standing position before recommencing walking, and acknowledging *right goes thus… left goes thus.*

4. When you reach the end of the walking path, stop. Acknowledge *standing… standing… standing* and then make your clockwise turn in three stages (six movements), with *turning* acknowledgements. You should already have practised the turning procedure and your turning movements should bring you facing back down the path, with your feet about three inches apart.

5. Acknowledge *standing… standing… standing* for a few moments and then commence walking, acknowledging *right goes thus… left goes thus.* Continue walking up and down the path, acknowledging the turns at each end, until the end of your practice time.

6. Your sitting meditation place should already be prepared with a cushion, if necessary. If the sitting place is in the same general area as the walking path, move mindfully to the sitting place, continuing to acknowledge *right goes thus... left goes thus.* When you reach the sitting place, stand for a few moments acknowledging *standing... standing... standing.*

7. Change from the standing position to the sitting position, as you have already practised. In Exercise 1, there is no need to overburden yourself by making acknowledgements of intentions of movement, but try to acknowledge as many movements as possible when changing position: *bending... lowering... grasping* etc. Introduce *intending to...* acknowledgements gradually over the weeks, as and when you feel you can concentrate sufficiently to do so.

Sitting meditation

Optimum duration: 30 minutes (or your own shorter, pre-set time).
Main acknowledgements: *rising... falling* (or *breathing in... breathing out*). Plus acknowledgement of external sensory stimuli, physical feelings, and mental formations.

In the first sitting exercise, you will be concentrating mindfulness on the rising and falling of the abdomen, plus acknowledging any external sensory stimuli (such as sounds), physical feelings that arise in the body (such as aches and pains) and thoughts or feelings that arise in the mind. If you need to move during this exercise – to change position, or to scratch at an itch, whatever – try to acknowledge the movements of the body, but don't worry in this exercise about acknowledging intention of movement.

Follow this procedure:

1. If you have just completed a period of walking meditation, you will already be in your sitting position. Adjust the cushions and your body as required, acknowledging *fidgeting... fidgeting* (or *moving... moving*).

2. Slowly close the eyes, acknowledging *closing*.

3. Move your awareness to an imagined circle about two inches across, just below the navel. As the abdomen rises, acknowledge *rising* as many times as necessary to cover the entire period of the movement. As the abdomen falls, acknowledge *falling*. Each acknowledgement <u>must</u> cover the entire rise and fall.

4. After only a few moments, you may well find that your concentration is no longer on the rising and falling of the abdomen, and you have been distracted by a sound, smell, some physical discomfort, or by some random thought that has arisen in the mind. Immediately acknowledge as appropriate and return concentration to the rising and falling of the abdomen. This will certainly happen many times, but try not to become impatient or frustrated at your lack of control over your mind. Just acknowledge each time and return awareness to the rise and fall of the abdomen. Continue to the end of your pre-set time until your alarm clock rings (don't forget to acknowledge *hearing... hearing*). Cease acknowledging the rising and falling of the abdomen.

5. Slowly raise your right hand from your lap and place it on your right knee, acknowledging each movement: *raising... moving... lowering... touching.* Slowly move the left hand to the left knee. Remember that each acknowledgement must cover the entire action, so you should not be acknowledging *moving* if the hand is still being raised.
6. After contemplating 'metta' for a few minutes, slowly open the eyes, acknowledging *opening... opening* and then *seeing.*
7. For a few moments, be aware of the whole body in the sitting position, acknowledging *sitting... sitting... sitting.*
8. Rise slowly from the sitting position to the standing position, acknowledging as many movements as you can. Stand still for a few moments, with your arms hanging by your sides, acknowledging *standing.*
9. Although your sitting meditation is now complete, you should continue to move mindfully, acknowledging each movement, until you have to begin to move normally again.

Lying meditation

Duration: start about 15 minutes before your normal sleep time and continue until asleep.

Main acknowledgements: *rising... falling* (or *breathing in... breathing out*). Plus acknowledgement of external sensory stimuli, physical feelings, and mental formations.

If you do not intend preceding lying meditation with a short period of walking meditation, start a mindfulness exercise from the moment you enter the bedroom. Acknowledge all your movements in the room, including getting undressed, getting onto or into the bed, and settling into the chosen position.

Apart from the position, lying meditation follows the same procedure as sitting practice. When in the lying position, move the awareness to the imagined abdominal circle and begin to acknowledge *rising... falling.* The mind can be quite busy at the end of the day, so it is likely your concentration will very quickly be distracted by random thoughts and memories of the day's events. Acknowledge each thought or distraction as usual, and return awareness to the rise and fall of the abdomen.

If you feel yourself becoming sleepy, do not try to force yourself to stay awake to complete a pre-set meditation time. Acknowledge *sleepy* and return to the rise and fall of the abdomen. Continue to acknowledge for as long as you can.

Mindfulness exercise

Optimum duration: about 30 minutes, though several shorter exercises can be practised instead.

Main acknowledgements: all movements, plus try to acknowledge as many intentions of movement as possible.

Subject: eating a meal.

'Eating a meal' is presented here as the first mindfulness exercise, but the exercises given at the end of this chapter can be practised in any order. Do not practise the same exercise more than 3 or 4 times successively. Instead, choose a variety of activities to practise within each of the exercise sections, perhaps choosing shorter exercises to start off with. Some suggested mindfulness exercises are given at the end of this chapter, but you can treat *any* activity as an exercise in mindfulness. The main point is to undertake the activity with total awareness.

The movements and acknowledgements given in the exercises are a guide only. You should not arrange your movements around the acknowledgements given. Carry out the activity of the exercise in your own style, and make your own acknowledgements accordingly.

In this exercise you have just sat down at the table and have a plate of food in front of you. As you look at the food, acknowledge *seeing... seeing*. Acknowledge *intending to eat... intending to eat*. Before you reach for the knife and fork, acknowledge *intending to reach... intending to reach*. As you reach for the knife and fork, *reaching... reaching... grasping... lifting... lowering*. As you cut the food and lift the fork to the mouth, *cutting... cutting... lifting... lifting... bringing... bringing*. As you place the food in your mouth, and lower the fork, *placing... lowering... closing... chewing... chewing*. As the taste buds recognise the taste of the food being chewed, *knowing... knowing... swallowing*. During the meal, if you reach for the condiments, acknowledge accordingly, *intending to reach... intending to reach... reaching... bringing... shaking... reaching... reaching... placing*. Similarly, if you reach for a glass of water, *intending to reach... intending to reach... reaching... reaching... lifting... lifting... opening... swallowing... lowering... placing...* etc.*

---

* **IMPORTANT:** *Before proceeding to Exercise 2, make an objective review of your progress of working with Exercise 1. If your mindfulness does not seem to have improved noticeably over the weeks or months, continue with Exercise 1 for a longer period, but practise walking meditation from Exercise 2 to help increase your concentration.*

Exercise 2

Walking meditation (2ⁿᵈ stage)

Optimum duration: 40 minutes (or your own shorter pre-set time)
Main acknowledgements: *standing... intending to walk... lifting... treading... intending to turn... turning.* Plus acknowledgement of sitting down movements before commencing sitting meditation.

Each new exercise introduces a new stage of walking meditation, but the earlier stages must also be practised so that concentration is built up gradually.

Walking meditation in Exercise 2 is in two parts, commencing with the stage one movements, as described in Exercise 1.

Stage 1: 20 minutes (or half of your own total pre-set walking period): *standing... right goes thus... left goes thus... turning.* At the end of the first period, on completion of a length of the path, and having made your turn, acknowledge *standing... standing... standing.*

Stage 2: 20 minutes (or half of your own pre-set walking period): *intending to walk... lifting... treading... standing... intending to turn... turning.*

In first stage walking meditation you kept awareness on only one movement of each foot – the moving forward movement. In second stage walking meditation, you will not acknowledge that movement at all, but instead will focus attention on two other movements: the lifting of the foot and the moment it touches the floor. The acknowledgement of the intention to walk, and the intention to turn, are also introduced in stage two.

After completing 20 minutes of first stage walking, follow this procedure:

1. You are facing down your walking path and have acknowledged *standing* as often as you need. Now, concentrate entirely on your intention to start walking, acknowledging *intending to walk... intending to walk*. Because of the concentration you have already built up during first stage walking, you may be very aware of your body as it tenses and prepares to move.

2. Lift the right foot. When the foot is lifted, the knee is first slightly bent and the heel rises from the floor. At this point the foot should be lifted about five inches from the floor without changing its downward angle. The acknowledgement *lifting* is made when the entire foot has left the floor and is in movement upwards – not from when the heel comes up alone. The foot should not be moved forward while the *lifting* acknowledgement is being made.

3. Move the foot forward a short pace and lower it to the floor. Make no acknowledgement either of the forward movement, nor of the lowering movement. The heel will touch the floor momentarily before the rest of the foot. The acknowledgement *treading* should be made as the heel touches the floor, but the acknowledgement should be made slowly enough to cover the entire placing of the foot onto the floor. Meanwhile, there should have been no movement in the left foot at all.

4. Follow the same procedure with the left foot and continue to the end of the walking path.

5. When you reach the end of the path, stop walking and acknowledge *standing*. Fully know that you intend to turn, as you make the acknowledgement *intending to turn... intending to turn.*
6. Make the turning movements and acknowledgements until you are facing back down the path. Acknowledge *standing* as necessary and then *intending to walk... intending to walk... intending to walk.* Commence walking, acknowledging the lifting and treading movements, until the end of the walking meditation period. Come to a final standing position at your sitting meditation place.

In second stage walking meditation, you may find that your pace is faster than in the first stage, but do not sacrifice mindfulness for speed; there is no need for speed. The lifting and treading movements can become very fluid and it is possible to become quite aware of the amount of energy involved in the movements, especially in treading. As the foot treads flat to the ground, the arches of the sole of the foot flatten to absorb the pressure of several thousands pounds per square inch. As the foot is raised in the lifting movement, the 'elastic' arch springs back into shape, returning about 17% of the energy to the movement.

Sitting meditation

Optimum duration: 40 minutes (or your own shorter pre-set time).
Main acknowledgements: *rising... falling... sitting.* Plus acknowledgements of intentions to move, movements, external sensory stimuli, physical feelings, and mental formations.

In Exercise 2, the acknowledgements *rising... falling* are extended to *rising... falling... sitting.*

If you mentally examine the rise and fall of the abdomen when breathing at a normal, relaxed rate, you will notice there is a space, or momentary stillness, between each fall and the next rise. During that space, you will now become aware of the whole body in the sitting position, using the acknowledgement *sitting* to help focus your awareness. Let awareness encompass the <u>whole body</u> as you make the acknowledgment, and not any individual area of the body. (You will be acknowledging specific areas of the body in later exercises). Do not acknowledge *I am sitting,* only *sitting.* If it helps, let an image of the body in the sitting position flash momentarily into your mind, as though seeing it in a mirror. The awareness and acknowledgement must be simultaneous, and only in the space between the fall and next rise of the abdomen.

Follow the same overall procedure of Exercise 1, but now also acknowledge as many intentions of movements as you can: *intending to close,* for example, before closing the eyes, *intending to open* before opening the eyes at the end of the sitting period, *intending to move, intending to scratch, intending to stand,* etc. Remember that *intending to* acknowledgements must be made and completed before the actual movement is started.

Lying meditation

Duration: 15-30 minutes.

Main acknowledgements: *rising... falling... lying.* Plus acknowledgements of intention to move, movements, external sensory stimuli, physical feelings, and mental formations.

Follow the same procedure as in Exercise 1, but now also be aware of the body in the lying position and acknowledge it in the space between the fall of the abdomen and the next rise. Also now acknowledge any intention of movement, as well as the movement itself.

Mindfulness exercise

Optimum duration: 30-40 minutes.

Choose any Mindfulness exercise, or combination of short exercises, from the suggestions given at the end of this chapter to make up an approximately equal time to your sitting practice.*

---

* **IMPORTANT:** *After working with Exercise 2 for at least one month, you should be capable of practising for the optimum times given. If, you make an objective assessment of your progress and developing mindfulness, and you feel you are not yet fully capable, continue to practise Exercise 2 before moving on to Exercise 3. To help increase concentration, practise third stage walking meditation with Exercise 2. The exercises now become increasingly more complex and a far greater level of concentration is required. The procedure in later walking exercises does not specify standing, turning, intending to walk, intending to turn. These should now be taken as standard procedure in all your meditation.*

Exercise 3

Walking meditation (3rd stage)

Duration: 45 minutes.
Main acknowledgements: *lifting... moving... treading.* Plus standard acknowledgements.

Stage 1: 15 minutes: *right goes thus... left goes thus.*
Stage 2: 15 minutes: *lifting... treading.*
Stage 3: 15 minutes: *lifting... moving... treading.*

In Exercise 3 walking meditation you will practise stages one and two for 15 minutes each. When you have made the last turn at the end of the second stage, acknowledge *standing* and *intending to walk* as usual.

In third stage walking meditation, there are three movements to be acknowledged for each foot: *lifting* and *treading* are the same movements that you have already practised in stage two. In stage three, as soon as the lifting movement is completed, move the foot forward a short pace whilst acknowledging *moving*. Do not start to lower the foot until the forward movement and acknowledgement are completed. Lower the foot, allowing the heel to touch the floor surface first, and, as soon as it does, acknowledge *treading*.

The acknowledgements of the individual movements must be very precise and you need to be totally mindful to ensure that you are making the acknowledgements at the right moment. From stage three walking onwards, it can be helpful to pause momentarily between each movement. This gives the walking motion almost a robotic quality, but it does help ensure that the physical movements and mental acknowledgements are perfectly synchronised, which is more important than fluidity.

Sitting meditation

Duration: 45 minutes.

Main acknowledgements: *rising... falling... sitting... touching.* Plus acknowledgements of intentions to move, movements, external sensory stimuli, physical feelings, and mental formations.

The new sitting acknowledgement *touching* is introduced in Exercise 3. *Touching* is the momentary awareness of the point of contact between one part of the body against the floor or cushion. The area of momentary awareness may be imagined as a circle about two inches across, and in Exercise 3 is located in the right buttock at the point where you can most feel pressure against the cushion or floor surface.

The awareness and acknowledgement of the touching point must be simultaneous, and must come immediately after the sitting acknowledgement, and before the abdomen begins to rise. If you breathe naturally quite fast, you may find that you must make the acknowledgements *sitting* and *touching* very quickly to fit them into the space between the fall and the next rise. Do not alter your breathing speed, nor forcibly hold the abdomen at the end of its fall to make more 'space' – your mind is perfectly capable of moving quickly from its visualisation of the sitting position to the awareness of the touching point. If it seems not to be, then you may not be ready to practise Exercise 3.

Lying meditation

Duration: 15-30 minutes.

Main acknowledgements: *rising... falling... lying... touching.* Plus acknowledgement of intentions to move, movements, external sensory stimuli, physical feelings, and mental formations.

In Exercise 3 lying meditation, the *touching* point is an area about two inches across on the right hip, at the point where there is most pressure between the hip and the bed surface.

If lying on the back, the *touching* point is the right shoulder against the bed surface.

Mindfulness exercise

Optimum duration: 30-40 minutes.

Although the mindfulness exercises are not detailed, they should be continued as part of your regular meditation programme. Choose exercises from the suggestions listed, or any other activity that you regularly undertake.

Exercise 4

Walking meditation (4ᵗʰ stage)

Duration: 45 minutes.

Main acknowledgements: *heel up... lifting... moving... treading.*
Plus standard acknowledgements.

Stage 1: 10 minutes: *right goes thus... left goes thus.*
Stage 2: 10 minutes: *lifting... treading.*
Stage 3: 10 minutes: *lifting... moving... treading.*
Stage 4: 15 minutes: *heel up... lifting... moving... treading.*

The acknowledgement *heel up* is introduced in fourth stage walking meditation and you will now be focusing awareness on four movements of each foot. Practise the first three stages of walking meditation for ten minutes each before coming to an *intending to walk* point at one end of the path. In fourth stage walking, acknowledge *heel up* at the precise moment the heel is raised from the floor. The toes and forward part of the foot should still be flat on the floor, and the *heel up* movement and acknowledgement must be complete before the rest of the foot is moved.

Remember that concentration levels must be built up slowly and it is important that the earlier stages of walking meditation should be practised before including the new stage.

Sitting meditation

Duration: 45 minutes.

Main acknowledgements: *rising... falling... sitting... touching* (2).
Plus acknowledgement of intentions to move, movements, external sensory stimuli, physical feelings, and mental formations.

The sitting practice now becomes more complex, but by this point your concentration level should be sufficiently high to undertake more demanding meditation. If it is not, continue with Exercise 3 for a longer period, but include fourth stage walking meditation.

In Exercise 4, *touching* is at two points – the right buttock, and the left buttock. Follow this sequence:

1. *rising... falling... sitting... touching* (right buttock).
2. *rising... falling... sitting... touching* (left buttock).
3. *rising... falling... sitting... touching* (right buttock) etc.

Lying meditation

Duration: until asleep.

Main acknowledgements: *rising... falling... lying... touching* (2).
Plus acknowledgement of intention to move, movements, external sensory stimuli, physical feelings, and mental formations.

As with the sitting practice, you will now alternate awareness of *touching* between two points. If lying on the side, the touching points are the right hip, then the left knee as it rests on the right knee. Follow this sequence:

1. *rising... falling... lying... touching* (right hip).
2. *rising... falling... lying... touching* (left knee).
3. *rising... falling... lying... touching* (right hip) etc.

If lying on the back, follow this sequence:

1. *rising... falling... lying... touching* (right shoulder).
2. *rising... falling... lying... touching* (left heel).
3. *rising... falling... lying... touching* (right shoulder) etc.

Exercise 5

Walking meditation (5th stage)

Duration: 45 minutes.

Main acknowledgements: *heel up... lifting... moving... lowering... touching.* Plus standard acknowledgements.

Stage 1:   5 minutes: *right goes thus... left goes thus.*
Stage 2:   5 minutes: *lifting... treading.*
Stage 3:   10 minutes: *lifting... moving... treading.*
Stage 4:   10 minutes: *heel up... lifting... moving... treading.*
Stage 5:   15 minutes: *heel up... lifting... moving... lowering... touching.*

The acknowledgement *lowering* is introduced in fifth stage walking meditation. It is very important that the acknowledgement is made exactly while the foot is in motion downwards, and the acknowledgement must be completed before any part of the foot touches the floor.

From stage 5, the acknowledgement *touching* replaces *treading*. *Touching* is acknowledged only at the moment the heel touches the floor surface, and should not be 'stretched' to cover the touching of the rest of the foot to the floor – *touching* refers only to the heel.

Sitting meditation

Duration: 45 minutes.

Main acknowledgements: *rising... falling... sitting... touching* (3). Plus acknowledgement of intentions to move, movements, external stimuli, physical feelings, and mental formations.

There are now three *touching* points to be acknowledged, in the following sequence:
1. *rising... falling... sitting... touching* (right buttock).
2. *rising... falling... sitting... touching* (left buttock).
3. *rising... falling... sitting... touching* (right knee).
4. *rising... falling... sitting... touching* (right buttock) etc.

Lying meditation

Duration: 15-30 minutes.

Main acknowledgements: *rising... falling... lying... touching* (3). Plus acknowledgement of intentions to move, movements, external stimuli, physical feelings, and mental formations.

The sequence if lying on the side is:
1. *rising... falling... lying... touching* (right hip).
2. *rising... falling... lying... touching* (left knee).
3. *rising... falling... lying... touching* (right shoulder).
4. *rising... falling... lying... touching* (right hip) etc.

If lying on the back, the sequence is:
1. *rising... falling... lying... touching* (right shoulder).
2. *rising... falling... lying... touching* (left heel).
3. *rising... falling... lying... touching* (left shoulder).
4. *rising... falling... lying... touching* (right shoulder) etc.

Exercise 6

Walking meditation (6th stage)

Duration: 50 minutes.

Main acknowledgements: *heel up... lifting... moving... lowering... touching... pressing.* Plus standard acknowledgements.

Stage 1: 5 minutes: *right goes thus... left goes thus.*

Stage 2: 5 minutes: *lifting... treading.*

Stage 3: 5 minutes: *lifting... moving... treading.*

Stage 4: 10 minutes: *heel up... lifting... moving... treading.*

Stage 5: 10 minutes: *heel up... lifting... moving... lowering... touching.*

Stage 6: 15 minutes: *heel up... lifting... moving... lowering... touching... pressing.*

Sixth stage walking meditation is the most advanced level. The action of 'pressing' is one of the most positive movements in walking meditation because it involves the feel of the surface beneath the foot, the feel of the weight of the body on the foot, and the relief of the weight as the next 'heel up' movement is made. Concentration levels can become very deep whilst observing and acknowledging this movement.

Sitting meditation

Duration: 50 minutes.

Main acknowledgements: *rising... falling... sitting... touching* (5). Plus acknowledgement of intentions to move, movement, external sensory stimuli, physical feelings and mental formations.

Sitting meditation now includes five *touching* points, in the following sequence:

1. *rising... falling... sitting... touching* (right buttock).
2. *rising... falling... sitting... touching* (left buttock).
3. *rising... falling... sitting... touching* (right knee).
4. *rising... falling... sitting... touching* (left knee).
5. *rising... falling... sitting... touching* (right ankle).
6. *rising... falling... sitting... touching* (right buttock) etc.

Lying meditation

Duration: 15-30 minutes.

Main acknowledgements: *rising... falling... lying... touching* (5). Plus acknowledgement of intentions to move, movement, external stimuli, physical feelings, and mental formations.

If lying on your side, the sequence of touching points is:

1. *rising... falling... lying... touching* (right hip).
2. *rising... falling... lying... touching* (left knee).
3. *rising... falling... lying... touching* (right shoulder).
4. *rising... falling... lying... touching* (left shoulder).
5. *rising... falling... lying... touching* (hand supporting head).
6. *rising... falling... lying... touching* (right hip) etc.

If lying on the back, the sequence is:

1. *rising... falling... lying... touching* (right shoulder).
2. *rising... falling... lying... touching* (left heel).
3. *rising... falling... lying... touching* (left shoulder).
4. *rising... falling... lying... touching* (right heel).
5. *rising... falling... lying... touching* (right hand).
6. *rising... falling... lying... touching* (right shoulder) etc.

Exercise 7

Walking meditation (6th stage)

Duration: 60 minutes.
Main acknowledgements: as in Exercise 6, plus standard acknowledgements.

You are now practising walking meditation in six stages, but it is important to remember that all stages should be practised in the sequence given in Exercise 6 before commencing your sitting meditation.

If you are practising without the guidance of an instructor, remember that the time spent in walking meditation should be equal to the time spent in sitting. With the periods shown in Exercise 7, that would mean a total of two hours spent in a continuous period of meditation. If this is not practical, then divide your total available time in two, equally for walking and sitting, and then further divide the walking meditation time into six periods. Do not exclude the earlier stages, but shorten them in the same approximate ratio as for Exercise 6. Even a couple of minutes concentrating on *right goes thus... left goes thus* is valuable before moving on to later stages.

Sitting meditation

Duration: 60 minutes.
Main acknowledgements: *rising... falling... sitting... touching* (7). Plus acknowledgement of intentions to move, movements, external stimuli, physical feelings, and mental formations.

In this final exercise two additional touching points are recognised and acknowledged. One is the touching of the left ankle against the floor or cushion, the other is awareness of <u>all</u> touching points as a group. This is not the same as the *sitting* acknowledgement, which is an awareness of the position, not of the sensation or feeling of 'touching'. Do not flash awareness from one point to another – you must try to be aware of the sense of touching as one experience. The sequence is:

1. *rising... falling... sitting... touching* (right buttock).
2. *rising... falling... sitting... touching* (left buttock).
3. *rising... falling... sitting... touching* (right knee).
4. *rising... falling... sitting... touching* (left knee).
5. *rising... falling... sitting... touching* (right ankle).
6. *rising... falling... sitting... touching* (left ankle).
7. *rising... falling... sitting... touching* (all points as one).
8. *rising... falling... sitting... touching* (right buttock) etc.

Lying meditation

Duration: until asleep.
Main acknowledgements: *rising... falling... lying... touching* (6). Plus acknowledgement of intentions to move, movement, external sensory stimuli, physical feelings, and mental formations.

The awareness of 'touching' at all points is now introduced into the lying position. The sequence if lying on the side is:

1. *rising... falling... lying... touching* (right hip).
2. *rising... falling... lying... touching* (left knee).
3. *rising... falling... lying... touching* (right shoulder).
4. *rising... falling... lying... touching* (left shoulder).
5. *rising... falling... lying... touching* (hand supporting head).

6. *rising... falling... lying... touching* (all points as one).
7. *rising... falling... lying... touching* (right hip) etc.

If lying on the back, the sequence is:

1. *rising... falling... lying... touching* (right shoulder).
2. *rising... falling... lying... touching* (left heel).
3. *rising... falling... lying... touching* (left shoulder).
4. *rising... falling... lying... touching* (right heel).
5. *rising... falling... lying... touching* (right hand).
6. *rising... falling... lying... touching* (all points as one).
7. *rising... falling... lying... touching* (right hip) etc.

Mindfulness exercises

In these mindfulness exercises, the practitioner should acknowledge all intentions to move and all movements. Acknowledgement of an intention must always precede the movement and must never overlap into the movement itself.

The following suggestions are activities of various lengths, but you can also choose any routine or mundane activity of your own to practise as concentration meditation. The activity should be of the type that you usually undertake automatically, or semi-automatically, and into which you usually do not need to put much thought, rather than an activity that you find personally interesting, or which holds your attention.

The movements and acknowledgements given in the examples are a guide only. In practice, you should undertake the activity in your own style and acknowledge accordingly.

Washing up

Some people feel real aversion to washing up, but there is nothing about it that should cause such aversion. It is just as it is – any aversion felt is just 'I' prejudice: "*I* hate washing up". If you feel such aversion to washing up (or to any other activity) this is also a good method in which to examine the way your mind works, sometimes.

In this exercise, be aware of your movements and intentions, and also of the sensory perceptions: the 'feel' of things. Be aware of the soapiness of the water, its temperature, the feel of the dishes when they are greasy, and again when they are clean.

When washing up, the dirty dishes may first be placed in the sink, or a bowl. Then the taps are turned on. Washing up liquid is added to the water and stirred around. The taps are turned off and we reach for a dishcloth or pad. The hands are placed in the water to feel the temperature, then the dishes are cleaned, rinsed, and placed on the draining board. You might make movements and acknowledgements like these:

Lifting... lowering... placing... lifting... lowering... placing... lifting... lowering... placing... feeling... feeling... greasy... greasy. Intending to reach... intending to reach... reaching... turning... turning. Intending to reach... reaching... reaching... bringing... bringing. Intending to squeeze... squeezing... squeezing... reaching... placing. Feeling... feeling... knowing. Reaching... reaching... bringing... lowering. Intending to wash... intending to wash... washing... washing... washing. Lifting... rinsing... rinsing... reaching... placing... returning... washing... washing... etc.

If you have an automatic dish-washer, there are just as many intentions and movements that can be made in loading and unloading the machine.

Taking a bath or shower

In taking a bath, you first open the bathroom door, then close and lock it behind you. The taps are turned on and whilst waiting for the bath to fill, you may then undress. The temperature of the water is tested and you may add bath salts before getting into the water. After washing, you get out of the bath, reach for towel and dry off before getting dressed again.

You might make movements and mental acknowledgements like these:

Intending to open... opening... opening... closing... closing... locking. Moving... moving... stopping. Intending to reach... intending to reach... reaching... turning... turning. Intending to undress... intending to undress. Raising... pulling... unbuttoning... removing... folding... folding... bending... removing... removing... folding... folding. Intending to bathe... intending to bathe... intending to bathe. Moving... lifting... lowering... knowing... lifting... lowering... sitting. Intending to wash... intending to wash. Reaching... reaching... bringing... lathering... lathering... washing... washing. Intending to stand... intending to stand... rising... rising... rising... standing... standing. Stepping... stepping... lowering. Intending to dry... intending to dry... reaching... reaching...grasping... bringing... bringing... drying... drying... bending... drying... raising... drying. Intending to dress... intending to dress... etc.

Dialling a phone number

In this short exercise, you might think first of the number you need to dial, then reach for the phone, pick it up, listen for the dialling tone, and press the keyboard.

Intending to phone... intending to phone. Thinking... thinking... knowing. Intending to reach... intending to reach... reaching... reaching... touching... touching. Intending to lift... intending to lift. Lifting... lifting... bringing... bringing... hearing... hearing. Intending to dial... intending to dial... pressing... pressing. Waiting... hearing... hearing... intending to speak... intending to speak.

Switching on a TV

In turning on a television, you might make these movements and acknowledgements:

Sitting... sitting... sitting. Intending to stand... intending to stand... rising... rising... standing... standing. Moving... moving. Intending to reach... intending to reach... reaching... reaching... pressing... seeing... hearing... changing. Intending to move... moving... moving... intending to sit... sitting... sitting.

Other suggested activities

1. Making a cup of tea or coffee.
2. Getting dressed or undressed.
3. Applying make-up.
4. Shaving.
5. Cooking a meal.
6. Cleaning shoes.
7. Moving a piece of furniture.
8. Loading and unloading a washing machine.
9. Washing or polishing a car.
10. Ironing a shirt or blouse.

Suggested further reading

A Constitution for Living. Ven P. A. Payutto, published by Buddhadhamma Foundation, Bangkok, Thailand.

Buddhism: An Introduction and Guide. Christmas Humphreys Published by Penquin Books.

Buddhism Explained. Ven Khantipalo. Silkworm Books, Chiang Mai, Thailand.

Dependent Origination: The Buddhist Law of Conditionality. Ven P. A. Payutto, published by Buddhadhamma Foundation, Bangkok, Thailand.

Entering the stream: An Introduction to the Buddha and His Teachings. Edited by Samual Bercholz and Sherab Chodzin Kohn. Published by Shambala Publications.

Good, Evil and Beyond: Kamma in the Buddha's Teaching. Ven P. A. Payutto. Published by Buddhadhamma Foundation, Bangkok, Thailand.

Mindfulness: the Path to the Deathless. Ven Acharn Sumedho. Published (for free distribution) by Amaravati Publications, UK.

The Four Noble Truths. Ven Acharn Sumedho. Published (for free distribution) by Amaravati Publications, UK.

What the Buddha taught. Walpola Rahula. Published by Wisdom Books.

World Faiths: Buddhism. Clive Erricker. Published by Hodder Headline.

English/Pali glossary

Absorbtion States, trance, ecstasy — Jhana

Aggregates of consciousness — Vinnana

Aggregates of matter (or form) — Rupa

Aggregates of mental functions — Sankhara

Aggregates of perceptions — Sanna

Aggregates of sensations — Vedana

Aversion (anger, ill-will) — Dosa

Buddhist monk — Bhikkhu

Causal continuity — Pattica-samuppada

Community of Buddhist monks — Sangha

Compassion — Karuna

Concentration — Samadhi

Concentration (Calmness) Meditation — Samatha

Contemplation of feelings — Vedananupassana

Contemplation of mental objects — Dhammanupassana

Contemplation of the body — Kayanupassana

Contemplation of the mind — Cittanupassana

Craving, thirst, desire — Tanha

Delusion — Moha

Equanimity	Upekkha
Eventual goal of Buddhists:	Nibbana
the extinction of all defilements and	
suffering. The Unconditioned	
Five Aggregates	Khanda (lit: heaps)
Five Hindrances	Panca nirvarana
(1) sensous lust	Kamacchanda
(2) ill will, hatred, anger	Vyapada
(3) physical and mental torpor	Thina-middha
(4) restlessness and worry	Uddhacca-kukkucca
(5) sceptical doubts	Vicikiccha
Four States of Consciousness	Brahmavihara
Greed	Lobha
Impermanence	Anicca
Insight Meditation	Vipassana
Insight-Wisdom	Vipassana
Intentional action	Kamma
Loving-kindness/ universal good will	Metta
Meditation	Bhavana (lit: mental development/culture)
Meditation on the in and out breaths	Anapanasati
Meditation positions	Mudra
Mental phenomena	Nimitta (lit: sign, omen, mark, portent)
Mindfulness	Sati
Morality	Sila
Natural Truths. Also,	Dhamma ('that which supports')
The Doctrine, The Teachings of the	
Buddha, the Truth, phenomenon,	
a cognisable object.	
No-self, soul-less	Anatta
One-pointedness of mind	Cittekaggata
Passing away of the Buddha	Parinirvana (lit: fully blown out)
Rebirth (Rebecoming)	Punabbhava
Relative Truth	Sammutti-sacca
Result of intentional action	Kamma-vipaka

Right Action	Samma kammanta
Right Concentration	Samma samadhi
Right Effort	Samma vayama
Right Livelihood	Samma ajiva
Right Mindfulness	Samma sati
Right Speech	Samma vaca
Right Thought	Samma sankappa
Right Understanding	Samma ditthi
Setting in Motion the Wheel of Truth Discourse	Dhammacakkappavattana Sutta
School of the Elders/ The Southern School of Buddhism	Theravada
(School of) The Great Vehicle/ The Northern School of Buddhism.	Mahayana
Suffering, misery, discomfort etc	Dukkha
Sympathetic joy	Mudita
The arising of Dukkha	Dukkha-samudaya
The cessation of Dukkha	Dukkha-nirodha
The Eight Precepts	Attha-sila
The Four Noble Truths	Cattari Ariyasaccani
The Five Precepts	Panca-sila
The Four Foundations of Mindfulness Discourse	Maha Satipatthana Sutta
The Middle Path of Practice	Majjhimapattipada
The Noble Eightfold Path	Ariya-atthangika-magga
The Triple Gem/ The Three Jewels	Ratanattaya
The way to the cessation of Dukkha	Dukkha-nirodhagamini-pattipada
Three Characteristics of Existence, the Three Signs of Being (also called the Common Characteristics)	Tilakkhana
Ultimate Truth	Paramattha-sacca
Unwholesome (unskillful, unwise)	Akusula
Wholesome (skillful, wise)	Kusala
Wisdom	Panna

The author's royalties from sales of this book are dedicated to

Phra Peter Pannapadipo's Students' Education Trust

A fund was established in 1994 by Phra Peter's friends in the UK to help a particularly disadvantaged Thai student who had gained a university place but could not afford the fees. More than enough was donated, so the balance became the foundation of a Trust Fund (SET) dedicated to helping other impoverished Thai students in similar difficulties.

By the beginning of 2000, the Trust Fund had grown considerably and was supporting more than 200 students, most of them studying at universities and technical, vocational or agricultural colleges.

Nearly all SET-supported students are from very poor rice-farming families. Without SET's help, most would have been unable to take up their deserved university or college places. Some of those already in higher education would have been forced to drop out and return to work in the family rice paddies, or find some other mundane, dead-end job. With SET's support, the students are achieving — achieving something for themselves and for the future of their country.

SET helps students in different ways, depending on individual need. For example:

● New students who have passed entrance examinations for universities or colleges, but who cannot take up their places because of proven family poverty.

● Students already in higher education who may be forced to drop out, unable to afford further fees.

● Students who face some temporary difficulty or unexpected expense and who need support only for a term or two.

- Students who need support or grants of some other kind — for books, uniform, tools, travel or specialised educational aids.

- Students whose villages are a long distance from their city university or college, and who need somewhere closer to live. SET can locate free accommodation in monasteries, where students also receive free food.

- Some particularly impoverished students may need total support, including college fees, accommodation, grants for books, uniform, bus fares — even for the occasional haircut.

Whatever genuine help the student needs, SET tries to provide it. Students at university currently receive annual fee grants of 10,000 - 20,000 Baht, while those at technical, vocational and agricultural colleges receive at least 6,000 Baht annually. This is usually enough to cover term fees. Other grants may be made depending on individual needs, and after recommendation to Phra Peter by the university or college Welfare Department. SET works closely with welfare officers and teachers to ensure that all students who are supported meet SET's criteria of proven need plus proven diligence.

Higher or vocational education in Thailand is relatively inexpensive, but there are hundreds of thousands of bright, diligent and deserving students who cannot afford even the modest fees. The Students' Education Trust can help only a very few of these disadvantaged students, but wants to do all it can for as many as possible. Even a small donation goes a long way in education in Thailand and can make a big difference to the future of a bright boy or girl.

If you are interested in knowing more about the Students' Education Trust, and how you can help, please write to:

Phra Peter Pannapadipo, Wat Worranatbanpot, Thammavitee Road, Amphur Muang, Nakhon Sawan 60000, Thailand.

Also by Phra Peter Pannapadipo

Whether you have a deep interest in Buddhism and meditation or simply find a Caucasian Buddhist monk a curiosity, this is a book you shouldn't miss.

ISBN 974-228-004-5

5 1/2" x 8" 308 pp. Paperback.

Available at leading bookshops.

Or order online at:

www.bangkokpost.net/postbooks

Phra Farang:
An English Monk in Thailand

"Not the usual stuff." Andi Francis, Bangkok Metro Magazine.

"...a middle-aged English businessman describes his gradual metamorphosis into a practising Buddhist monk while being initiated into the intricacies of an unfamiliar Southeast Asian culture... This book offers a highly readable account of beginning again and realistically points out the pitfalls and rewards for the Westerner who chooses to follow the path of the Buddhist monk in Thailand." James Pruess, The Bangkok Post.

"A delightful little book that should be read by anyone with an interest in the practice of Buddhism... sparkles with humorous anecdotes, which the author relates in a self-deprecating manner, since in every case he is the butt of the joke." William Page, The Nation.

"Look within, for thou art Buddha."

Good morning,
Buddha

by the author of Phra Farang: An English Monk in Thailand
Phra Peter Pannapadipo

ISBN 974-228-005-3
5 1/2" x 8" 212 pp. Paperback.
Available at leading bookshops.
Or order online at:
www.bangkokpost.net/postbooks

Good morning, Buddha

Buddha — a fully-awakened one — is not confined to the altar, immortalised in bronze or gold, remote and untouchable.

The qualities that make a Buddha do not come from "out there" but are already "within" each of us. To uncover them, it is necessary to make the practice of Buddhism part of our everyday life, the basis of our every thought, word and action. And this is what *Good morning, Buddha* is all about.

Written by Phra Peter Pannapadipo, the author of *Phra Farang: An English Monk in Thailand* and *One Step at a Time: Buddhist Meditation for Absolute Beginners*, *Good morning, Buddha* propounds that Buddhist philosophy is of little value in our daily lives if we approach it intellectually. Rather we have to *do it* and *live it* for it to have any real value and to reap the benefits.

Based on the author's discourses with visitors and groups of students, *Good morning, Buddha* explains the concept of Buddha and the practice of Buddhism in simple and practical terms, using the author's lay life experiences and current issues as case studies. The author does not seek to present the Buddha's teaching in its entirety nor in any particular order. Rather his topmost concern is how lay people can use the teaching in a practical way to help them in this life, regardless of whether they are Buddhists or simply seeking a moral and ethical code or a philosophy to lead them into the future with confidence.

READ MORE IN POST BOOKS

For complete information about books available from Post Books and
how to order them, write to us or visit our website at the following address:
Post Books, The Post Publishing Plc. 136 Na Ranong Road,
off Sunthorn Kosa Road, Klong Toey, Bangkok 10110, Thailand.
Tel: (662) 240-3700 ext. 1691-2 Fax: (662) 671-9698
e-mail: postbooks@bangkokpost.co.th   http: //www.bangkokpost.net/postbooks

Softcovers:

The White Umbrella   Patricia Elliott   *5" 1/2 x 7"—404 pp.—1999*
A dazzling true tale of modern Burma told through the life story of a woman
who has been called Princess, Mahadevi, First Lady, MP, rebel leader and refugee...
Her journey — from quiet Shan hills to the presidential palace in Rangoon to
the halls of power in Asia and Europe; and finally to the violent, drug-laden
netherworld of the Golden Triangle — is a revelation about Burma, Southeast
Asia, and about what happens when the games of superpowers are played out
of real life. With a pro-logue by Bertil Lintner, maps and B/W photographs.

The Black Swan   Anthony Aikman   *4" 1/2 x 7" 1/8—146 pp.—1999*
The plight of homeless Cambodian children and the fate of their turbulent country
provide a backdrop for the tale. Full of allusions and ironies, this illustrated book
is in effect a philosophical debate. Thought-provoking yet easy to read, it looks
into the very nature of human being.

PostScript: Forgotten But Not Gone   Roger Crutchley
5" x 7" 1/2—188 pp.—1999
"No more trivia." is a warning to Roger Cruthley's fans, "Get ready to tackle the
serious issues facing Thailand head on." And that is exactly what he does, address-
ing only the really important matters in life in his second book which includes
potholes, pickled parrots, squashed lizard and men with bald heads!

Thai Ways   Denis Segaller   *5" x 7"—248 pp.—2000—7th printing*
An informative and enjoyable book which articulates very succinctly much that
is Thai in custom and tradition. It plays a significant part in encouraging the
non-Thai as well as Thai readers to better understand and appreciate the intricacies that comprise Thailand.

More Thai Ways   Denis Segaller   *5" x 7"—250 pp.—2000—5th printing*
A sequel to the best-selling *Thai Ways*. The book covers a host of subjects from
ceremonies, customs, to Thai language, legendary animals, sheding light into
the fascinating background of the Thai ways of life.